AT THE CONTROLS

AT THE CONTROLS

The Smithsonian National Air and Space Museum Book of Cockpits

PHOTOGRAPHY BY ERIC F. LONG AND MARK A. AVINO
Edited by Tom Alison and Dana Bell

Smithsonian National Air and Space Museum, Washington, D.C.
in association with

The BOSTON
MILLS PRESS

A Boston Mills Press Book

Copyright © 2006 The Smithsonian Institution

First paperback printing

Publisher Cataloging-in-Publication Data (U.S.)

At the controls : the Smithsonian National Air and Space Museum book of cockpits / photography by
Eric F. Long and Mark A. Avino ; edited by Tom Alison and Dana Bell.

[144] p. : ill. (chiefly col.) ;   cm.
Includes bibliographical references.

ISBN-13: 978-1-55046-482-5
ISBN-10: 1-55046-482-5

1. Airplanes — Cockpits — Pictorial works.   2. Airplanes — Cockpits — Catalogs.   3. Airplanes —
Washington (D.C.) – Pictorial works.   4. National Air and Space Museum — Catalogs.
I. Long, Eric F., 1954-   II. Avino, Mark A., 1959-   Alison, Tom, 1941-   III. Bell, Dana.
IV. National Air and Space Museum.   V. Title.

629.135   dc22   TL681.C6A88 2006

Library and Archives Canada Cataloguing in Publication

Long, Eric F., 1954-
At the controls : the Smithsonian National Air and Space Museum
book of cockpits / photography by Eric F. Long and Mark A. Avino ; edited
by Tom Alison and Dana Bell.

Includes bibliographical references.
ISBN 1-55046-365-9 (bound).—ISBN 1-55046-482-5 (pbk.)

1. Airplanes—Cockpits—Pictorial works.   2. Airplanes—Cockpits.
3. Airplanes—Washington (D.C.)—Pictorial works.   4. Smithsonian National
Air and Space Museum.   I. Avino, Mark A., 1959-   II. Alison, Tom, 1941-
III. Bell, Dana, 1950-   IV. Smithsonian National Air and Space Museum
V. Title.

TL681.C6L65 2001   629.135   C2001-901814-2

ISBN-13: 978-1-55046-482-5
ISBN-10: 1-55046-482-5

Published by Boston Mills Press
132 Main Street, Erin, Ontario N0B 1T0
Tel: 519-833-2407 Fax: 519-833-2195
e-mail: books@bostonmillspress.com

In the United States:
Distributed by Firefly Books (U.S.) Inc.
P.O. Box 1338, Ellicott Station
Buffalo, New York 14205

In Canada:
Distributed by Firefly Books Ltd.
66 Leek Crescent
Richmond Hill, Ontario, Canada L4B 1H1

*The publisher gratefully acknowledges the financial support for our publishing program by the Canada
Council for the Arts, the Ontario Arts Council and the Government of Canada through the Book
Publishing Industry Development Program*

Design by PageWave Graphics Inc.

Printed in China

This book is dedicated to the men and women, past and present,
of the Paul E. Garber Facility in Suitland, Maryland,
who work daily to preserve, store, catalog and
archive the collections of the
National Air and Space Museum.
Their dedication to the duties they perform
behind the scenes is an inspiration to all of us
whose passion for aviation and history is displayed
within the walls of the Smithsonian and museums across the country.

Contents

Foreword

Almost everyone likes to look at airplanes, especially warbirds and antiques. But whether you see them flying overhead or on the ground at air shows, you can see only the exteriors — the cockpits remain an intriguing mystery. At Oshkosh and Sun and Fun, where you are allowed to view the airplanes up close, people are constantly seen on tiptoe, craning their necks to see into the cockpits. Here at the National Air and Space Museum, where we have the world's premier collection of historic aircraft, visitors are not permitted to get that close, so they are denied even a glimpse of the cockpit. We have tried to place mirrors strategically in an attempt to solve this problem, but the difficulty of placing the mirrors and the issue of reversed images made this an unsatisfactory solution.

The public's fascination with cockpits was illustrated rather forcefully for me when I was commanding Marine Aircraft Group 11 at El Toro, California. During a weekend open house, I had an F-4 Phantom placed on the ramp with the cockpit open to allow visitors to climb in and be photographed. So many people were lined up awaiting their turn that I had to add three more Phantoms to satisfy the demand. I could understand their attraction, since as a boy I spent many happy hours sitting in the cockpits of Marine F4U Corsairs in my father's group. Since then, many of the most satisfying hours of my life have been spent in the cockpits of Marine aircraft.

It is interesting to note that the complexity of aircraft cockpits increases almost directly with their performance. Compare the cockpit photographs of the World War I SPAD XIII, the World War II P-51D Mustang, the Gulf War F-16 Fighting Falcon, and the Space Shuttle *Columbia*. Their respective top speeds are 130 mph, 437mph, 1,320 mph, and 17,500 mph. Imagine the reaction of a SPAD pilot who is put into the cockpit of an F-16. After being overawed and even frustrated by the myriad dials, screens, switches and levers, he would start to feel a sense of familiarity as he recognized some basic controls and instruments: control stick (albeit, side-mounted in the F-16), rudder pedals, and throttle, compass, altimeter, and airspeed indicator. Some version of these are found in almost all types of piloted aircraft.

Those of you who may never have the opportunity to sit in the cockpits of historic or commonplace aircraft may find solace in *At the Controls*. I believe this to the be the finest collection of cockpit photographs in existence. You will see the cockpit from the point of view of the pilot, with access not only to the instrument panel, but the consoles as well. This is due to the meticulous preparation and great skill of NASM photographers Eric Long and Mark Avino. The writing is equally good, with clear, concise descriptions of the aircrafts' histories and precise identification of the instruments. Tom Alison is a veteran pilot with almost 1,000 hours in the SR-71 Blackbird, while Dana Bell is a widely recognized author and expert on aircraft markings. This book will be a valuable and much-used addition to your library.

Jack Dailey, Director
National Air and Space Museum
Smithsonian Institution

Photographers' Introduction

As photographers for the Smithsonian's National Air and Space Museum, we have the distinct opportunity of photographing collections associated with aviation and space history, ranging from pieces of artifacts to full-size aircraft. Many are one-of-a-kind and are exclusive to our collection. From the Wright Flyer to the SR-71 Blackbird and, more recently, NASA's Space Shuttle *Columbia*, we are challenged to document these artifacts creatively. *At the Controls* is our look at a selection of these famous artifacts. By using creative lighting techniques and an extremely wide-angle lens mounted on a 4-by-5-inch camera, we have duplicated the sensation of being at the controls inside the cockpit.

The Camera

We decided to shoot with the widest angle lens available, using the largest format camera we could find. That format, 4 x 5, came in an architectural camera called a Cambo Wide. Marketed through Calumet Photographic, the camera was loaned to us by Calumet (and eventually purchased) to experiment in shooting wide, open spaces and small spaces needing wide coverage. The camera is basically a lens and back, and measures a depth of five inches. Shorter than any other 4 x 5 available at the time, it enabled us to work in extremely confined spaces. The camera is supplied with a 47 mm XL Super Angulon lens, covering 120 degrees, equivalent to a 13 mm lens on a 35 mm camera. The lens is supplied with a helical mount, allowing the lens to focus exactly like a 35 mm camera. The focusing mount has markings in feet and meters, with f/stops labeled on the lens barrel. We avoided the use of a fisheye lens on a medium-format camera because of the accentuated distortion characteristic of a fisheye lens. We did try using a fisheye in one cockpit, the *Friendship 7* capsule. The capsule's

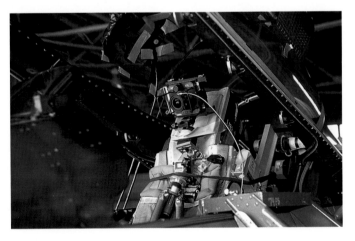

extremely cramped space proved difficult to access with our 4 x 5 camera, though it is the 4 x 5 image that we used in the book. We removed the helmet and head of the mannequin inside *Friendship 7* to gain the perspective of being in front of the controls. Similarly, we needed to remove the mannequin of Orville from the Wright Flyer in order to shoot what little there is of the cockpit of the first powered plane to fly.

The illustration shows the camera mounted on a tripod and strapped to the seat back; in this case, the cockpit of an F-16C. Our camera, a first-generation model, did not have a revolving back. It was modified by our machinists at the Paul E. Garber Facility to accommodate a tripod plate on the vertical axis and thus allow transition from horizontal to vertical shots. In virtually all cockpits, the camera needed to be "zone" focused. As mentioned earlier, the lens mount is marked with distances in feet and meters, and f/stops are marked on the lens barrel. By measuring the closest and furthest points in the cockpit, we were able to match these distances to the f/stops on the lens barrel to see if the aperture used would cover the distance needed. F/stop coverage is also called depth of field, the ability of the f/stop used on the lens to cover distances from close to far. Generally, the more distance, or depth, needed, the smaller the f/stop. F/16 will not cover as great a depth as f/32. For example, at f/16, this lens will cover distances from three and a half feet to infinity. At f/32, the distance increases from two feet to infinity. Most of the cockpits photographed needed coverage of a distance somewhere between one foot and five feet. When zone focused, using one foot for the closest setting reduces the furthest point covered to four feet when set at f/32.

Wide-angle lenses have one unfortunate drawback: distortion. This lens gave the impression of roominess even in the tightest of spaces. The edges of the frame are also "stretched" due to the wide coverage, a tradeoff in being able to capture a wide perspective. The illustration also shows unconventional aids that allowed us to level or straighten the camera. The roll of 120 film shoved under the tripod handle permitted a perspective change when rotating the camera was not possible. Once strapped in, dense foam was sandwiched between the tripod and seat to allow clearances for Polaroid and film backs, keeping the camera taut at the same time. Extreme care was employed when securing the camera, as we had to make sure not to damage the artifact. In only one case, when shooting inside the Russian Soyuz capsule, were we unable to secure the camera mounted to the tripod and therefore forced to hand-hold the unit during exposures while sitting inside the capsule.

Lighting

The key to photographing any object is lighting. Controlling the light source is crucial to image creativity. In the majority of aircraft, we were challenged by having to creatively light each cockpit. Additionally, we needed to be careful with the heat of the light source and its effect on the fragile museum pieces. The shooting conditions and the control of ambient light dictated the lighting used, whether electronic flash or tungsten (quartz), each having advantages and disadvantages.

We used Speedatron Black Line and Elinchrom 1000 EL electronic flash units. Electronic flashes had the advantage of fan-cooled light units, but they were difficult to control, especially when minor lighting adjustments were necessary. Electronic flash also makes bracketing of exposures difficult. As stated earlier, when an extreme f/stop, such as f/32, is required to cover depth of field, bracketing exposures with strobes is only possible by changing the f/stop or the intensity of light. Changing the f/stop also affects the depth of field, and changing the intensity of the strobe light proved difficult. In cases where more light was needed but unmanageable, we would "push" the film to give us the extra light we required, increasing the ASA of the film from 100 to 200. We would then change the processing of the film to accommodate the change in film speed.

Tungsten light, on the other hand, offers greater control of the light source as well as the ability to bracket exposures using exposure time rather than intensity or f/stop. Most exposures ranged between thirty seconds and one minute. The disadvantage of tungsten lights is the heat from the light source. We also needed absolute darkness, since ambient or existing light would affect the color balance of the film. We used Mole Richardson Mini Spot lighting fixtures, each using a 200-watt FEV bulb balanced for 3200 K tungsten film. These lights are focusable from broad to spot and have

many accessories to control the light sources. This small light source allowed controlled lighting, making needed fill or small changes in lighting easy. Unfortunately, the heat generated from these lights made for a few second-degree burns on the photographers' hands and necessitated our extreme caution while working within the confines of museum artifacts. Woods, metals, fabrics, plastics, and glass can all be affected by heat generated from these lights. In cases in which light was required inside the cockpits — under the seat, for example — we used a 200-watt bulb in the modeling light of a fan-cooled Speedatron head, which we could also disassemble to make for a small and effective fill. We could also dial down the intensity of the modeling light to provide the necessary amount of fill.

For the most part, we tried to duplicate the effect of sunlight illuminating the cockpit, filling the harsh shadows with soft fill light. We used Rosco Tough Rolux, a mylar diffusion material designed for intense heat from theatrical lights, to soften light, and 1- and 2-stop neutral density filters to reduce the intensity of light. We also used a black photographic tinfoil to shape the light where necessary. Designed for use with theatrical lights, this foil will not burn and proved an excellent resource when we needed to block or alter the shape of light, as stated earlier. Some aircraft dictated the kind of lighting effect we sought. The SR-71 Blackbird, a spy plane developed in the early 1960s, called for far more dramatic lighting to give the feel of a highly secretive plane.

Only three cockpits, those of the Space Shuttle *Columbia*, the F-16C, and the Airbus, provided their own power, enabling us to shoot these state-of-the-art cockpits "powered up." These cockpits also had computer, or "glass cockpits," with their own power sources to illuminate their screens. In our experience, computer screens generally look best photographed with daylight film with a 30 magenta filter. The Space Shuttle *Columbia*, shot in Palmdale, California, was lit with its internal emergency fluorescent lights, which were then diffused by mylar gels and pieces of black paper, thus adding a fill but not overpowering the computer screens. We also had the advantage that the seats had been removed from the cockpit, a decision NASA made prior to our arrival. The Shuttle shoot was complicated by technicians working on the aircraft as we were exposing film. With exposure times ranging between one and two minutes, movements within the Shuttle compounded our ability to make the necessary time exposures. As seen in the illustration, NASA also took precautions by dressing us in "bunny" suits so we wouldn't leave behind foreign debris. We also had to be careful not to leave behind scraps of gels, Polaroids, and other materials used to control lighting. Our film was processed by the NASA/Dryden Photo Lab to avoid the film being x-rayed by airport security. In these three cockpits, we used both daylight and tungsten films, not knowing for certain how cockpits would best be rendered. In the Airbus, the fluorescent lights used to add light to the cockpit were balanced for tungsten, even though the computer screens would best be seen with daylight film. The F-16C had computer-generated screens with tungsten lamps illuminating the dials.

One interesting note along these lines is that, unlike museum artifacts, the Shuttle, Airbus and F-16C are considered active aircraft. We had to be careful when working within these cockpits so as not to leave behind debris. When a binder clip was dropped inside the F-16 cockpit, not much concern was shown until our light meter was crushed by the canopy, and the maintenance chief appeared wanted to account for all missing pieces of the meter. It was then that the binder clip became a problem. Fortunately, the pilot helped us recover it.

Films

Three 4 x 5 films were shot exclusively on this project: Kodak E100S, Kodak 64T Tungsten, and Polaroid Type 55. Kodak E100S gave us excellent results for both short (flash) and long (timed) exposures, sometimes exceeding the recommended ninety-nine seconds. It also allowed us to increase film speed to 200 by push processing, yielding excellent results. Kodak 64T allowed for extremely long exposures (a characteristic of tungsten films) and bracketing exposures by changing time. Polaroid Type 55 permitted both short and very long time exposures, and produced a black-and-white print, allowing us to preview and make changes to our lighting and composition. This film also produced a black-and-white negative, allowing us to examine, through a loupe, the sharpness of the image. This was essential when zone focusing the lens and determining depth of field, as mentioned earlier.

Introduction

The cockpit of an airplane or spacecraft is where humanity and technology meet. It is where the pilot actually takes control of the machine. *At the Controls* gives the reader an opportunity to view the cockpits of a number of the aircraft and spacecraft in the Smithsonian Institution's National Air and Space Museum collections. Many of these historically significant craft are one of a kind, others are well known, even by non-aviation buffs, for significant events in mankind's travel through air and space history.

The wonderful cockpit images created by Smithsonian photographers Eric Long and Mark Avino are designed to give the reader an up-close-and-personal sense of just what the pilot's "office" looks like in each of these craft. The particular craft were chosen to give the reader a sense of the advances and changes in technology; from the very simple hip cradle and wing-warping control of Orville and Wilbur Wright's 1903 Flyer to the magnificently modern glass cockpit in the NASA Space Shuttle *Columbia*. As airplanes developed in terms of performance and capability, so did their cockpits and controls.

The origin of the use of the word *cockpit* to describe the area in which a pilot controls an airplane or spacecraft is difficult to pinpoint. The term was not used by the Wright Brothers when referring to the pilot's position in their Flyer, but by 1913 it was associated with the semi-enclosed area for pilots and passengers in aircraft having fuselages. Over time the term has evolved to one that specifically describes a position for pilots as they direct the flight of aircraft and spacecraft.

That evolution is revealed as we see the changes and improvements in the flight instruments, navigational instruments, and actual flight controls reflected in these unique photographs. Early aviators controlled their craft by sight, sound, and feel. Instruments and flight controls were rudimentary, and the airplane's reaction, slow — almost awkward by modern standards. As airplane engines increased in power, the craft's speed and performance also increased. Wood and fabric became aluminum alloy, and soon even stronger alloys, such as the titanium of the SR-71, were used. Today, we see high-strength composites as the common material in aircraft and spacecraft construction.

Airspeed and altitude measuring instruments evolved to be larger in scale and more precise. With the historic flight of the Bell X-1 in October 1947, when Captain Chuck Yeager first flew faster than the speed of sound, another term entered the pilot's lexicon, *Mach*, and another instrument, the *Mach meter*, became important. Later, we see these speed-measuring indicators developed from round analog instruments to digital readouts combined with other information on a glass screen, as in the cockpits of the F-16, the Airbus, and the Space Shuttle.

The attitude indicator made the pilot no longer dependent on visual confirmation of the airplane's position relative to the Earth; it also enabled the pilot to control the craft while in cloud or while otherwise unable to see past the front of the airplane. Early vacuum indicators became electrically operated, providing more reliability, and still later were developed to project their information on television-like screens, their input coming from an air data computer.

Early aviators navigated completely by reference to landmarks on the ground. One of the earliest navigational instruments was the small, non-precision, wet compass, enabling the pilot to determine the basic direction of flight. This evolution of instrumentation can also be followed in *At the Controls*, as heading indicators and radio compasses turn into flight directors and precision-instrument landing systems, and on to the sophisticated, satellite-based Global Positioning System, which indicates the aircraft's position within a matter of feet.

All the aircraft cockpits photographed for *At the Controls* are a part of the National Air and Space Museum's collection, with the exception of the F-16, the Airbus, and the Space Shuttle *Columbia*. Any treatment of the subject of cockpits should reflect current technological standards, thereby allowing the reader to measure the changes that have taken place over time. For this reason, we have included these three modern cockpits, even though the specific aircraft and spacecraft are not a part of the National Collection.

Whether the reader's interest is in the artistic aspects of aviation, its technical developments, historic significance, or simply a general curiosity about aviation and space flight, we trust that *At the Controls*, featuring the superb photographic work of Eric Long and Mark Avino, will be a source of pleasure, interest, and knowledge.

Acknowledgments

Patricia Jamison Graboske originated the idea for this book and shepherded it into being over five years. William B. Hanna saw its potential and signed it up for Stoddart Publishing Company. The staffs at Stoddart and Boston Mills Press, especially Matt Williams and Noel Hudson, turned raw materials into a finished product. Andrew Smith, Joseph Gisini and Kevin Cockburn at PageWave Graphics developed the book's design.

NASM Associate Director Dr. Ted A. Maxwell lent his backing to the book, bringing several departments to the table and providing funding to cover many of the project's costs. Gen. J. R. "Jack" Dailey, Director, and Donald S. Lopez, Deputy Director, enthusiastically supported this project. The Museum's Aeronautics and Space History divisions made the initial selection of the book's forty-five cockpits. The Bogen Photo Corporation provided Elinchrom equipment, and Calumet Photographic came through with the 4x5 Cambo Wide camera. At the Smithsonian's Office of Imaging, Printing and Photography, Jim Wallace, Lorie Aceto, Jeffrey Tinsley, and Larry Gates supplied the time, processing, equipment, and materials needed to create each photo. John Fulton, Bill Reese, and their staffs, particularly Charles Burton, Karl Heinzel, Matt Nazzaro, Edward Marshall, Lars McLamore, Robert McLean, and Bernard Poppert prepared many of the aircraft cockpits prior to shooting and offered the insights into the cockpit designs developed during their years working with the Museum's collections. Dave Heck, Cathleen S. Lewis, and Amanda Young provided access to the Museum's spacecraft.

Access to the F-16 was provided by Colonel Dana T. Atkins and the men and women of the U.S. Air Force's 20th Fighter Wing at Shaw Air Force Base, South Carolina. Special help came from Captain Ron Watrous, Wing Public Affairs Officer, and Captain T. J. Lowe and Airman Travis Ward of the 55th Fighter Squadron. Barb Hanson and Joanne Fluke of United Airlines arranged for the cockpit of one of their Airbus A 320s to be available. Julie Kramer White of the Engineering Directorate, NASA Johnson Space Center and Al Hoffman of Boeing Reusable Space Systems in Palmdale, CA, made the preparations for our Space Shuttle Columbia photo shoot, while Jim Ross at NASA's Dryden Flight Research Center provided the support of his photo lab. Betty Skelton Frankman and Patty Wagstaff provided additional information for their aircraft.

Spacecraft cockpit text was researched and prepared by Space History Division curators Cathleen S. Lewis, Valerie Neal, and Michael J. Neufeld. Support and guidance for the aircraft cockpit texts came from NASM's Aeronautics Division staff, including division chair Dominick A. Pisano, Dorothy S. Cochrane, Thomas J. Dietz, Von Hardesty, Peter L. Jakab, Russell E. Lee, and F. Robert van der Linden. Peter D'Anna researched and explained several aircraft cockpits, while the Garber Facility's Ed Mautner drafted the Ar 234 and Fw 190 pieces.

Photographic and documentary support came from the staff of the NASM Archives, including division chair Thomas F. Soapes, Marilyn Graskowiak, Dan Hagedorn, Kate Igoe, Allan Janus, Kristine L. Kaske. Melissa A. N. Keiser, Brian D. Nicklas, Paul Silbermann, David R. Schwartz, and Larry Wilson. Charles O. Hyman provided his expertise in reviewing image color. Additional photos of NASA spacecraft were provided by Ms Gwen Pitman of the Headquarters NASA Photographic Center.

Family support is always critical on a project as involved as this book. All of us recognize the extra effort from the "home front," particularly from Carolyn Alison, Laurene Avino, Susan Lawson-Bell, and Kathy Long.

To all these individuals and organizations, Eric, Mark, Tom, and Dana wish to extend their heartfelt thanks for helping to bring this book to fruition.

Wright Brothers 1903 Flyer

On December 17, 1903, the Wright Flyer became the first heavier-than-air, human-carrying aircraft to fly under its own power and its pilot's control. The aircraft was equipped with a surprisingly sophisticated cockpit — more advanced than many of its successors. But most of the Flyer's controls were designed to be adjusted on the ground, and its instruments were read only after each flight.

Launched from a dolly riding on a fixed rail, the Flyer was anchored with a cable while designers Orville and Wilbur Wright primed the pistons, opened the fuel valves, connected a portable battery, and hand-turned the twin propellers to start the engine. They then adjusted the fuel flow and engine timing, and removed the battery.

With the engine warmed up, Orville stretched out prone across the wing. The engine was to the right of the Flyer's centerline, and Orville to the left (making Orville the first pilot to fly from the "left seat"). His feet braced against a foot board, he positioned his hips within an open steering cradle. A short wooden handle in his left hand moved the elevators to change the aircraft's pitch.

Satisfied that all was ready, Orville released the restraining cable with his right hand, then grabbed a wooden spar for support as the Flyer started down the launch rail. The aircraft's three instruments were started simultaneously and automatically as a string connected to the launch rail tightened, pulled a single lever to the left, snapped, and fell away. This action pushed a Veedor counter against the crankshaft to

Wilbur Wright stands to the right as his brother, Orville, makes the first flight at Kitty Hawk, North Carolina, on December 17, 1903.

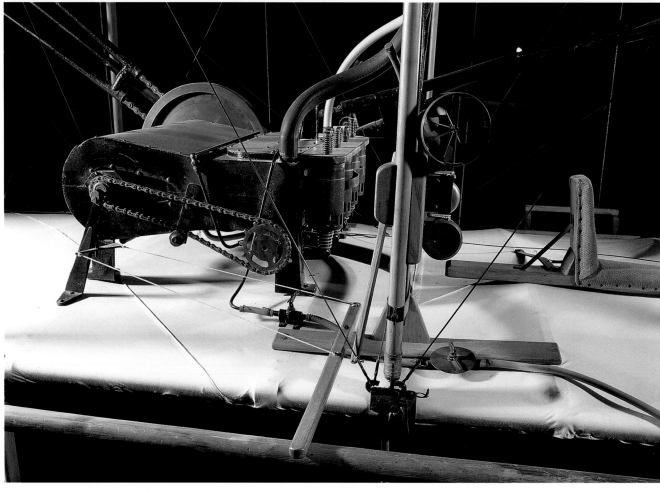

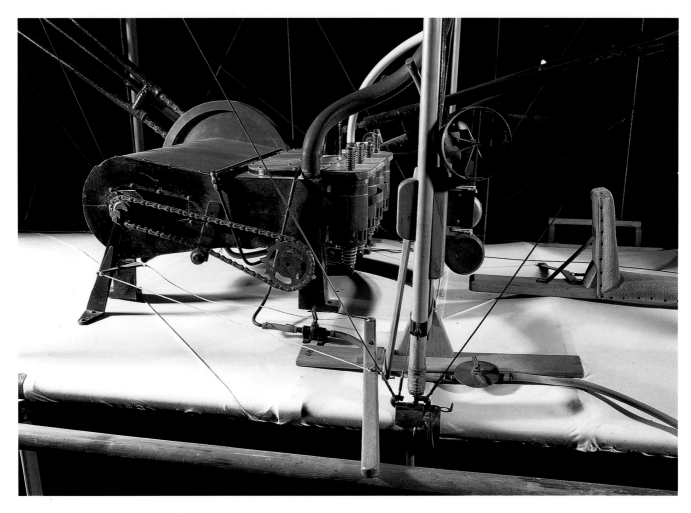

count engine revolutions, released the paddles of a French-built Richard anemometer to measure the distance traveled through the air, and started a stopwatch to measure flight time. As the Flyer bounced to earth a few seconds later, Orville threw the lever to the right, stopping the instruments and cutting the engine fuel supply. The successful first flight, however, also included history's first instrument failure: the hard landing zeroed the sensitive stopwatch, erasing the measured flight time. The brothers estimated a flight of twelve seconds and calculated their air speed, ground speed, and engine and prop revolutions per minute. Though the stopwatch failed on each of the day's landings, the brothers employed a hand-held backup to monitor each other for the remaining three flights.

The main photo looks forward from the pilot's footrest. Crossed cables connect the pilot's padded hip cradle to the outer wing panels and rudders — a quick shift of the hips to either side twisted outer wing panels and swiveled the rudders to bank and turn the Flyer. Beyond the hip cradle, a short wooden handle controlled the elevators (seen at the front of the fragile aircraft)

for climbing or diving. Mounted vertically on a strut beside the water stand pipe are (top to bottom) the small pinwheel of the Richard anemometer, the recalcitrant stopwatch, and the anemometer dial. The engine rests at the right.

Three inset photos show the Flyer's controls along the leading edge of the wing. A yellow fuel line snakes in from the lower right corner to the adjustable valve that served as throttle. (Though the valve was in easy reach of the pilot, it was adjusted only on the ground.) The line then passes beneath a board through an on/off valve and to the engine.

A black metal clip on the wing's leading edge held the restraining cable. To the left of the vertical strut, a wooden lever is shown in three positions. Before and after each flight, the lever was pushed toward the engine, shutting the main fuel valve and stopping all of the instruments (left top). During engine startup, the lever was centered, opening the fuel valve (left bottom). When pulled toward the pilot, the lever pressed a wooden actuator to start the anemometer and stopwatch (above). At the same time, a string pulled the revolution counter against the camshaft.

Blériot Type XI

Debuting in 1908, the Type XI would be Frenchman Louis Blériot's first successful monoplane. Following numerous successes in air meets and races, the Type XI drew international recognition in July 1909 when, with Blériot at the controls, it became the first airplane to cross the English Channel. Soon hundreds of Type XIs would be ordered, with dozens of imitations produced worldwide. Although technological advancements would soon surpass the Blériot XI, over 800 would be built and production would continue through 1914.

Delivered in July 1914, the NASM's Type XI was flown by Blériot's Swiss-born chief pilot, John Domenjoz. Following a demonstration tour of South America, Domenjoz brought the aircraft to New York in September 1915, thrilling crowds across the U.S. with his aerobatic maneuvers. Domenjoz returned to France in late 1916, but resumed his U.S. tour in 1919, flying his beloved Type XI at several additional American air shows.

Domenjoz's Blériot XI was powered by a 50-horsepower Gnôme Sigma rotary engine. The propeller was fixed to the front of the engine, with the prop and engine turning as one unit around a fixed shaft. Two tanks at the front of the cockpit held fuel, with the left tank partitioned to hold castor oil lubricant. Vertical sight gauges on the tanks indicated fuel and oil levels. A third tank, mounted beneath the engine, provided fuel during Domenjoz's trademark inverted flight maneuvers. The handle at the left side of the cockpit switched fuel flow from the lower tank and back again.

In 1908, there were no accepted standards for flight controls, and they varied greatly from designer to designer. Blériot's innovative cloche system, named for the bell-shaped housing at the base of most early examples, employed a single control stick and rudder pedals. Fore-and-aft movement of the stick shifted the elevators, bringing the nose up or down. Shifting the stick from side to side warped the wings, creating roll. Rudder movements, for yaw, resulted from pushing the pedals. (The "wheel" atop the control stick was a simple two-handed grip and did not turn.) As Blériot's aircraft became more popular, so did his control system, which remains in use a hundred years later.

The Blériot's rotary engine was started by manually turning the prop. With the engine started, the pilot adjusted fuel flow with the lever on the cockpit's right side and carburetor air with the small lever beneath the control stick handle. If the tachometer to the left of the cockpit indicated that the engine was operating at maximum speed, the Blériot was ready for takeoff; neither engine control would be adjusted in flight. The only in-flight engine adjustment came from the small white button atop the control stick. Pressing the button shorted the magneto, reducing speed for landing and producing the familiar *brupp, brupp* sound heard on so many pioneer aircraft. Once on the ground, the pilot cut the fuel supply, and the engine stopped.

John Domenjoz's newly restored Blériot Type XI, photographed at the Museum's Paul E. Garber Storage and Restoration Facility in 1979.

The Blériot XI's instruments gave only a rudimentary understanding of performance. A fuel pressure gauge was mounted to the left of the centerline, with an early pressure altimeter (missing from the aluminum housing seen in the photo) to the right. The small glass bulb of the oil pulsator (to the right of the altimeter) gave visual assurances that castor oil was pumping to the engine; counting the number of bubbles per minute served as a backup tachometer. Although compasses and clocks were not mounted in the Blériot XI, these items were often carried as personal equipment.

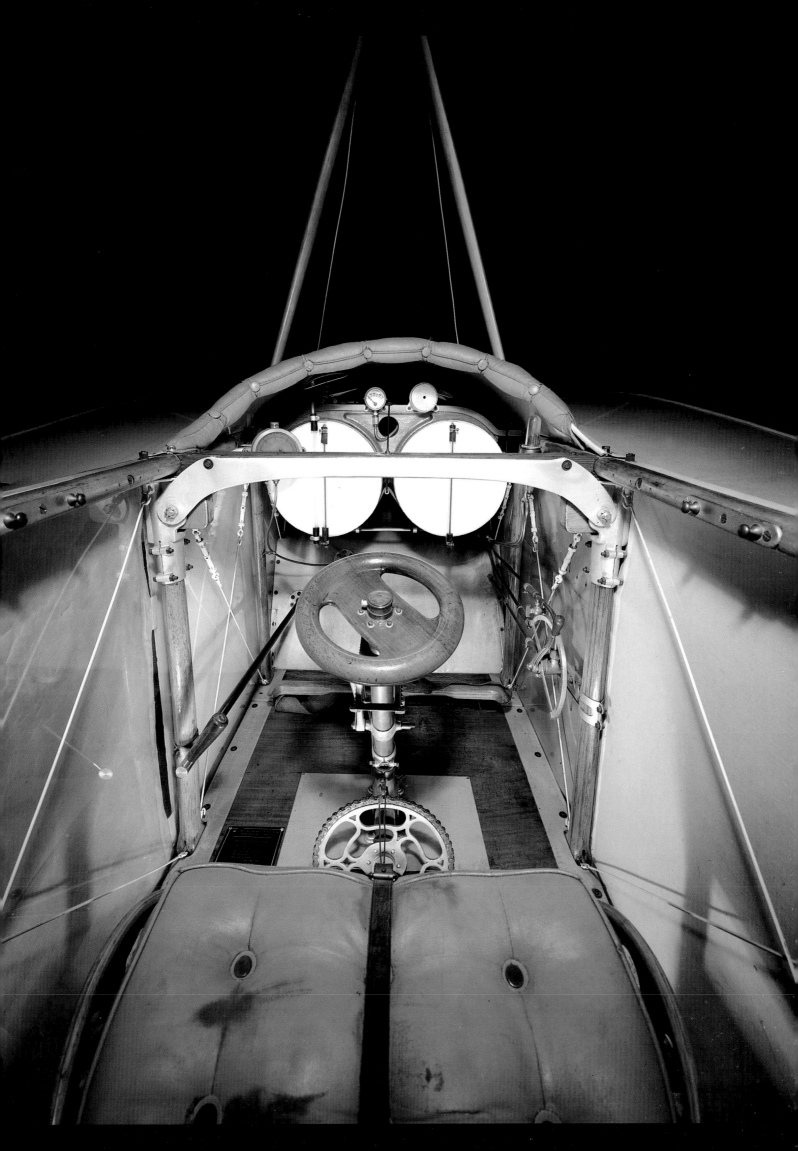

SPAD XIII *Smith IV*

When France's Armand Deperdussin began producing aircraft in 1910, Louis Blériot was already established as an aircraft builder. Deperdussin soon became known for a line of racing monoplanes and military scouts, and an innovative flight control system. The "Dep" system used rudder pedals and a control column with steering wheel. As with Blériot's controls, pitch was still controlled by fore and aft movement of the column, but roll was now manipulated by wheel rotation rather lateral stick movement. Although the name is long forgotten, today Dep controls are standard on many aircraft.

Despite his many successes, Deperdussin was jailed for fraud in 1913. Blériot soon took control of the company, which was renamed "SPAD" (erroneously thought to mean "speed" in the then-fashionable international language *Volapuk*). Contemporary company literature justified the new name as an acronym for *Société Anonyme pour l'Aviation et ses Derives*. Today, the name SPAD is best remembered for the company's most famous product, the SPAD XIII, which saw action in World War I. The United States purchased almost 900, including this example, which was flown over the Western Front by Lieutenant Arthur Raymond "Ray" Brooks.

Designed in 1917, the SPAD XIII was a *chasseur*, or fighter, with a primary mission of destroying enemy

An unarmed SPAD XIII of the 95th Aero Squadron, photographed in the U.S. shortly after the War.

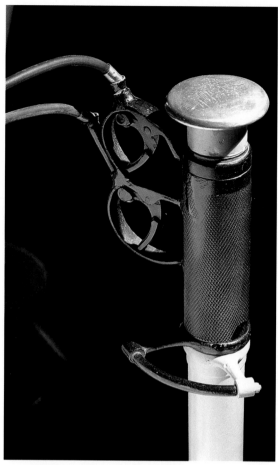

*Twin triggers on the control column allowed independent
firing of the SPAD's Marlin machine guns.*

aircraft. The aircraft carried twin 30-caliber Vickers machine guns fitted with interrupter gears to synchronize firing between the spinning propeller blades. Brooks replaced his Vickers with American-built Marlin guns, the butts of which are visible just below the windscreen. Although the Marlins ejected their spent cartridges to either side of the fuselage, Brooks's SPAD retained the two diagonally mounted aluminum chutes that had carried away the Vickers's cartridges.

Significantly, most other cockpit fixtures monitored or adjusted the 220-horsepower Hispano-Suiza engine. In the days before parachutes, engine loss in a SPAD XIII could prove fatal. As one American pilot complained, the aircraft glided like "a bloody brick." Three brass switches, mounted between the machine gun butts, controlled fuel tank pressurization. The magneto switches, oil- and fuel-tank pressure gauges, a tachometer, and a radiator temperature gauge were mounted on the shelf to the left. The fuel level in the main tank was measured by a floor-mounted gauge between the pilot's knees. (In the event of fire, a nearby release could jettison the entire tank, with the upper-wing reserve tank providing enough fuel for the pilot to land safely.) Forward movement of the large aluminum-handled

throttle (mounted to the pilot's left) increased engine speed. (The reverse would be true on many later French aircraft, with forward motion decreasing engine speed.) Behind the throttle, a smaller lever adjusted the carburetor fuel-air mixture; just above, a small knob opened and closed radiator shutters for engine cooling.

On the right shelf, an aluminum "spider bracket" carried a barometric altimeter; spring mounts dampened engine vibrations. At the center of the panel, a second spider bracket originally carried the aircraft clock. A compass, not seen in this view, was mounted to the left.

In common with most fighters, the SPAD XIII had a Blériot-style control stick, leaving the pilot's left hand free for the throttle. The standard rudder bar was fairly close — engine pumps foreshortened the cockpit — leading many pilots to complain of leg fatigue following long flights.

The Museum's SPAD XIII was damaged by German fighters during combat on October 30, 1918. Following repairs, mechanics painted small Maltese crosses where enemy bullets had hit the aircraft. The three crosses beneath the replacement windscreen apparently represented the three rounds that shattered the original.

Fokker D.VII

Dutchman Anthony Fokker moved to Germany in 1910, becoming involved in flying and aircraft design by the end of the year. Moderately successful before World War I, Fokker became famous for his fighter designs during the War. Earliest recognition came for a series of machine-gun-armed monoplanes first produced in 1915. In 1917, a new triplane design briefly controlled the skies. Finally, in February 1918, Fokker's D.VII biplane fighter was selected for production. By September, French SPAD XIII pilots were ordered to avoid combat with the new Fokker, which was found to be superior in all tactics except diving. Two months later, at the War's end, it was still considered the best fighter in production. Article IV of the Armistice agreement specified that Germany surrender certain aircraft, "especially all machines of the D.VII type."

The D.VII's superiority resulted from its sturdy, lightweight, steel-tube fuselage structure, its internally braced, wooden cantilever wings (which also eliminated the customary forest of drag-producing external bracing wires), its fine engines (though most pilots preferred the BMW engines to the less powerful Mercedes), and its clean, aerodynamic lines.

The wings and the fuselage were usually covered with a pre-printed lozenge camouflage fabric. (Enough dye generally bled through the fabric to be visible inside the cockpit.) German squadrons would paint aircraft noses and tails in unit colors, with individual motifs decorating

Nickchen IV was a Fokker D.VII flown by Fritz Blumenthal
of Jasta 53 (Fighter Squadron 53).

other areas. These "Flying Circus" markings were more than simple embellishments: since all inter-aircraft communications were visual (generally hand signals), conspicuous markings helped pilots recognize their units and comrades through formation and combat.

As with the SPAD XIII, most of the Fokker D.VII's cockpit instruments and controls related to the engine. The three switches at the base of the control panel (one to the left, two to the right) controlled pressurization of the fuel tanks in the same manner as the SPAD's three brass switches. A keyed magneto switch and a magneto starting switch were to the left of the panel, and a hand-operated engine lubricant pump to the right. At the center of the board, the tachometer was flanked by pressure gauges for the main and auxiliary fuel tanks; the hand pump to manually pressurize tanks was to the right beneath panel. The only other standard D.VII instrument, a compass, was most often mounted in the circular aluminum bracket seen just to the right of the seat.

The thin wooden handle to the pilot's left was the throttle, with a second lever, just forward, regulating the fuel/air mixture. A second throttle was mounted on the control column: the wooden knob at the left allowed the pilot to change his speed with both hands on the flight controls. The lever inside the larger wooden handle fired the twin 7.92 mm Spandau machine guns, which were synchronized to fire through the propeller arc. Cables between the pilot's feet led from the lightweight welded-steel rudder bar to the rudder.

Under the terms of the Armistice, the U.S. received a number of Fokker D.VIIs, but the Museum's example was captured shortly before the War's end when a pilot of Jasta 65 (Fighter Squadron 65) landed at a U.S. field in France. It was the Americans who mounted the airspeed anemometer (see inset) on the outer wing struts.

Bellanca C.F.

In late 1909, Sicilian Giuseppe Mario Bellanca, Enea Bossi, and Paolo Invernizzi designed, built, and flew the first Italian airplane, but that aircraft was destroyed in the crash that ended its first flight. In 1910, Bellanca designed and built a second aircraft, but, for want of an engine, it never flew. In 1911, after moving to New York with his family, Bellanca built and flew his first successful aircraft, and used it to teach himself to fly. Several new designs followed, each capable and well engineered, but none a financial success.

In June 1922, Bellanca's Model C.F. rolled out of its Omaha, Nebraska, factory. An astonishingly clean and efficient monoplane, the wood-and-fabric C.F. would win every competition it entered over the next fifteen months, often beating aircraft with four times the power. But despite its many successes and popular renown, only one Model C.F. would be built. The post-World War I market was flooded with inexpensive surplus aircraft; at twenty times the price of a surplus JN-4, the C.F. would be an engineering marvel but a commercial failure. The C.F. was ahead of its time, but it was the vanguard of a long line of Bellanca cabin monoplanes, a line that would find commercial success for decades to come.

The C.F.'s four passengers sat comfortably in an enclosed cabin, protected from the weather, noise, and exhaust. The pilot, however, sat behind them in an open cockpit, head exposed to the slipstream. This was no oversight on the designer's part; most contemporary pilots preferred an open cockpit, relying on their senses to navigate and to recognize danger signs from the aircraft and surroundings. While they were often correct, there was still much to understand about the disorienting effects of flight.

The Bellanca C.F., photographed following its restoration by the National Air and Space Museum in 1980.

Forward visibility was poor from the C.F. cockpit, which was set far aft. The pilot's view of the runway was blocked by the fuselage and thick wing. Yet pilot reports were glowing, suggesting that visibility was not the primary concern in contemporary aircraft. Bellanca originally offset the cockpit to the left, helping pilots to lean out for a glance beneath the left wing. Alternately, the pilot could duck his head into the cockpit and sneak a glimpse between the passengers through the side and front cabin windows.

Inside the cockpit, instruments and controls were rudimentary. The main panel, offset to the right, contained oil pressure and oil temperature gauges, a tachometer, and a magneto switch, all supporting the engine. The throttle and carburetor controls were originally mounted to the left. (These were missing when the aircraft was donated to the Museum and cannot be replaced without documentation of their original configuration.) The C.F. mounted no navigational instruments — not an uncommon arrangement in aircraft of the early 1920s. Flight controls were a simple joystick and rudder bar.

Without a radio, the C.F. pilot could not communicate with ground stations. (In the early 1920s, radios were still heavy, expensive novelties carried by few aircraft.) Communication with passengers was another matter. The pilot could easily duck his head to call out instructions at any time.

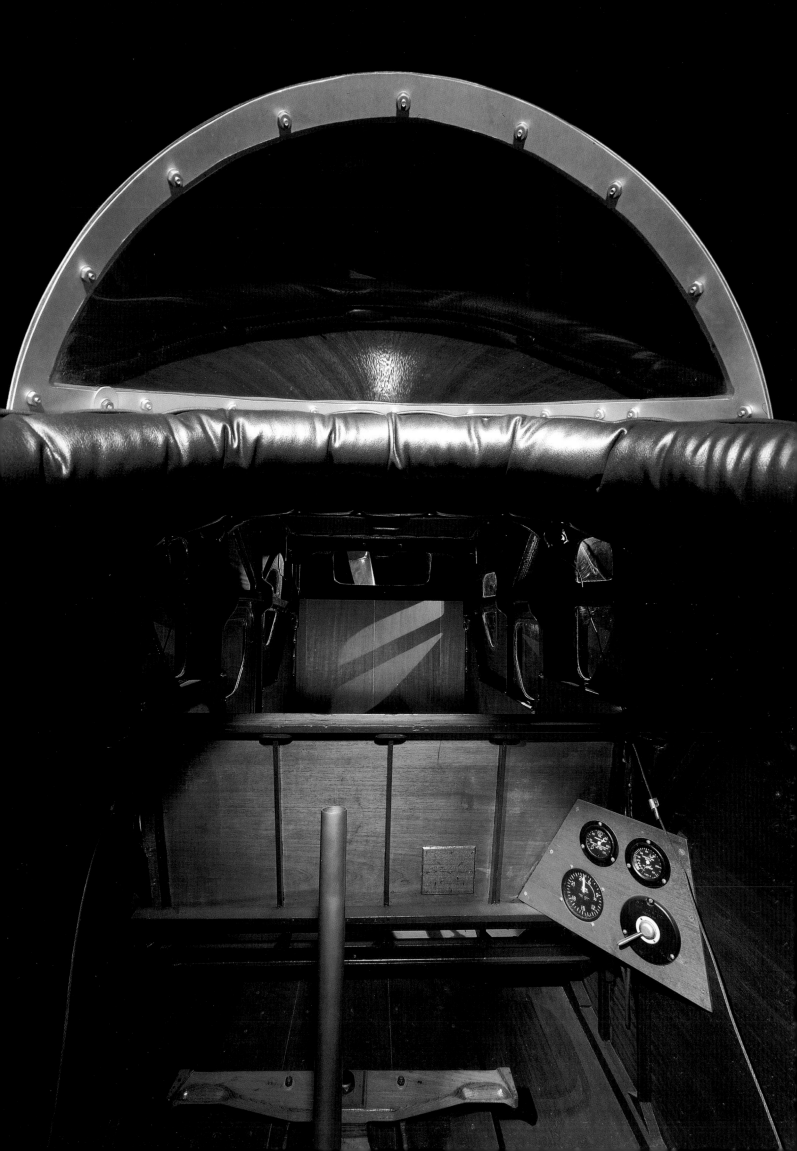

Douglas M-2 Mailplane

Unlike the innovative Bellanca C.F., the Douglas M-2 Mailplane was a conventional, externally braced biplane. It was also a commercial success, with fifty-nine built. The Mailplanes were derived from Douglas's successful line of O-2 military observation planes, a commonality that helped minimize development and production costs. The Mailplanes also used the O-2's proven 400-horsepower Liberty engine, which provided enough power to carry up to 1,000 pounds (450 kg) of cargo.

The U.S. Post Office purchased the first Douglas Mailplane (the DAM-1) in 1925, and Western Air Express (WAE) ordered five M-2 variants by the end of the year. In April 1926, WAE launched contract airmail service between Salt Lake City, Utah, and Los Angeles, California (via Las Vegas, Nevada), a distance of about 660 miles (1,060 km) covered in just over six hours. M-2s, and subsequent M-3s and M-4s, remained in service into 1930.

All six Douglas M-2s flew in the silver and red colors of Western Air Express.

When designing the Mailplanes, Douglas engineers put the pilot in the aft cockpit (where the observer/gunner sat in the O-2). The forward cockpit, reconfigured for cargo, was lined with sheet aluminum and asbestos for fire protection. (The pilot's cockpit had no such fireproofing!) When necessary, the cargo compartment could be configured for two passengers — upper hatches folded inward, removable seats were installed, and windshields were fitted.

NASM's Mailplane was an M-4 restored to flying condition as an M-2 by Western Airlines (WAE's descendant) in the 1970s. The Federal Aviation Administration would not certify the aircraft as airworthy until cockpit instrumentation was updated dramatically. (The standard cockpit of 1925 was hopelessly outdated

fifty-two years later.) Most of the original cockpit instruments were refitted before the aircraft went on display at NASM.

Instruments on the original main panel related primarily to engine functions: a tachometer, an oil temperature gauge, and an ammeter. A pressure altimeter was mounted at the right of the board, doubtless a comfort to pilots navigating the treacherous mountain passes between Salt Lake City and Los Angeles. Oddly, the airspeed indicator and compass were mounted in the forward cockpit. Perhaps this arrangement was a comfort to the occasional passenger, but neither instrument was easily visible from the pilot's seat.

Gauges for the two 60-gallon (227 L) fuel tanks were situated on either lower wing, above the tanks. The two gauges at the left of the cockpit were modern additions. Both tanks could be jettisoned in an emergency and fuel drawn from a 10-gallon (38 L) reserve tank in the upper wing. The right-side cockpit panel held electrical switches and fuses. A few of the switches were added when radios were required in the 1970s. Left-side controls included the throttle, fuel mixture (carburetor) controls, radiator shutters, fuel tank selector switches, and tail skid locking lever.

The Douglas Mailplanes required constant handling, leaving pilots few opportunities to take both hands off the control stick. To relieve arm strain, a large wheel at the left side of the pilot's seat adjusted the stabilizer; as fuel was consumed, changing the aircraft's center of gravity, minor stabilizer trimming could keep the nose level without adding more elevator. Rudder pedals were mounted on a central pivot, with cables leading back through the cockpit at either side of the stick.

Ryan NYP *Spirit of St. Louis*

In 1919, French-born American entrepreneur Raymond Orteig offered a $25,000 prize for the first nonstop flight between New York City and Paris. With the passing years, many would cross the Atlantic, but by 1927 none had successfully flown between the two great cities, and many of the world's most celebrated aviators were planning attempts. Airmail pilot Charles A. Lindbergh was not famous, but he convinced a group of businessmen from St. Louis, Missouri, to back his bid for the prize.

Lindbergh planned to fly alone in a single-engine aircraft. Unable to purchase the new Bellanca design that was his first choice, he commissioned a design from Ryan Airlines, a small firm in San Diego, California. In late February 1927, Ryan chief engineer Donald A. Hall, plant manager W. Hawley Bowlus, and a small crew began work on the new monoplane. Two months later, the Ryan NYP (for "New York to Paris") was ready. Lindbergh christened the aircraft the *Spirit of St. Louis*, began a series of test flights, and, between May 10 and 12, flew to New York, setting a new transcontinental record.

In New York, several other teams were preparing their aircraft and awaiting favorable weather. On the morning of May 20, 1927, Lindbergh took off. Thirty-three hours and thirty minutes later he landed in Paris, safely completing the 3,610-mile (5,810 km) journey.

Charles Lindbergh at the controls of the Spirit of St. Louis *prior to his flight from New York to Paris.*

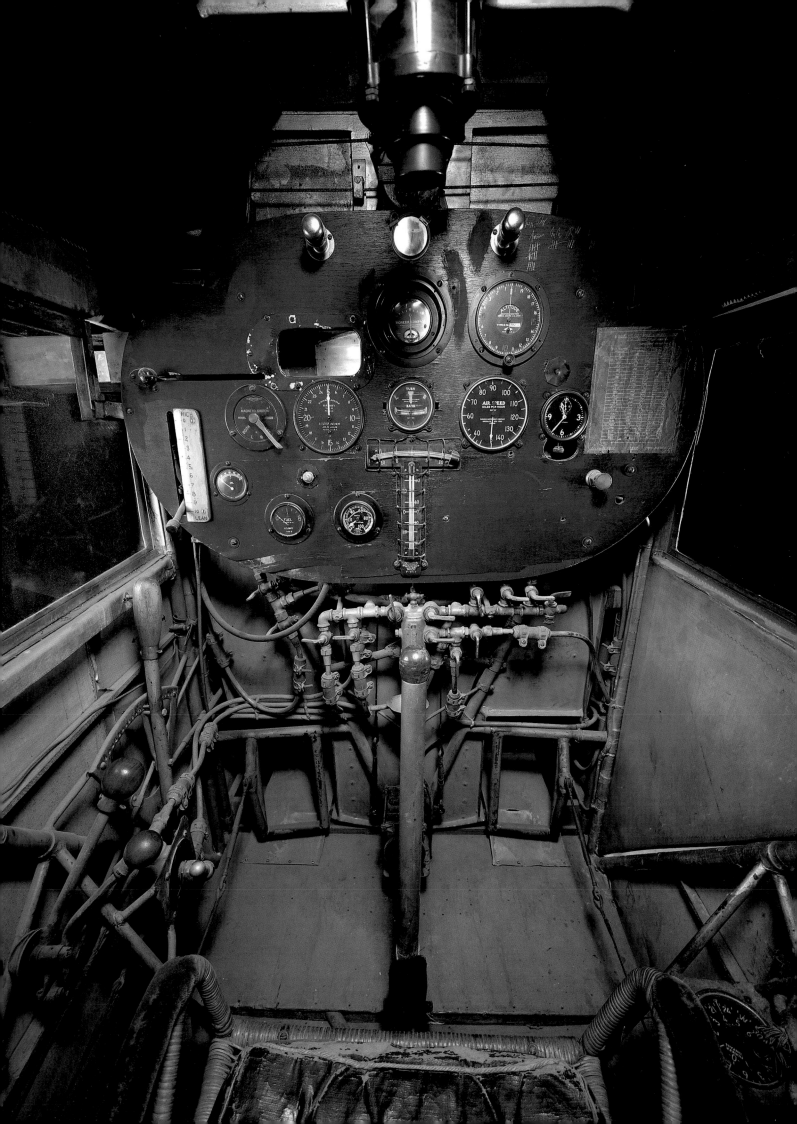

Few could have imagined the worldwide reaction to Lindbergh's flight. A combination of personality and accomplishment raised the young aviator to a status that few other flyers would ever share. Returning home, Lindbergh and the *Spirit of St. Louis* toured the U.S., Central America, and South America for several months. Lindbergh presented the aircraft to the Smithsonian in April 1928.

The *Spirit of St. Louis*'s cockpit was designed to its pilot's requirements. To avoid being crushed between the fuselage fuel tank and engine in the event of a crash, Lindbergh ordered the cockpit situated behind the tank. Although the tank completely blocked forward vision, Lindbergh was comfortable with the view through his periscope, which slid into position at the left side (see inset), or through his side windows. For the transatlantic flight, Lindbergh made his unheated cabin more uncomfortable by storing the two side windows behind his seat. On a 33-hour flight, comfort could lead to sleep, and sleep could be fatal!

The instrument panel included the best available instruments, not necessarily the newest. Lindbergh was looking for reliability, since most of his navigation would be based solely on those instruments. Centered above his head was a magnetic compass. Its numbers were reversed, read by their reflection in a mirror at the top of the panel. The readout for a second type of compass, an earth inductor compass, was directly below the mirror. When the course was dialed into the indicator at the pilot's right hip, the gauge on the instrument panel displayed any deviation from that course. A chart at the right of the panel tracked the expected hourly changes in magnetic declination (though the chart shown was not used for the New York-to-Paris trip). Just to the left, the aircraft clock tracked the passing of the hours. Above the chart is a penciled tally where Lindbergh tracked his hourly fuel consumption from each of his four tanks.

To help keep the aircraft level, Lindbergh used an inclinometer (the T-shaped gauge filled with green fluid) and, just above, a turn and bank indicator. An altimeter and airspeed indicator were just right of the panel center. Engine instruments, at the left side of the panel, completed the suite. The aircraft carried no radio, as Lindbergh preferred to save the weight to allow for extra fuel.

Lockheed Model 8 Sirius
Tingmissartoq

In September 1929, Charles Lindbergh evaluated the new Lockheed Air Express parasol at the National Air Races. Greatly impressed, he asked Lockheed chief engineer Jerry Vultee to design a low-wing, high-performance version for his use. This radical modification was well within Lockheed's capabilities: the Air Express, designed to replace Western Air Express's Douglas M-2s, was a parasol modification of Lockheed's Vega, just as the Explorer (originally designed for Arctic explorer Sir Hubert Wilkins) was a low-wing version.

The new aircraft, which Lockheed named the Model 8 Sirius, saw numerous small modifications before it was accepted on April 20, 1930, at Burbank, California. (Fourteen more Model 8s would subsequently be built for other customers.) Lindbergh and his seven-months-pregnant wife, Anne, then left for New York, stopping only once for fuel and setting a new transcontinental speed record.

By mid-1931, the Sirius had been modified, its original 450-horsepower Pratt & Whitney Wasp engine

Charles and Anne Lindbergh's Sirius, seen in 1931.

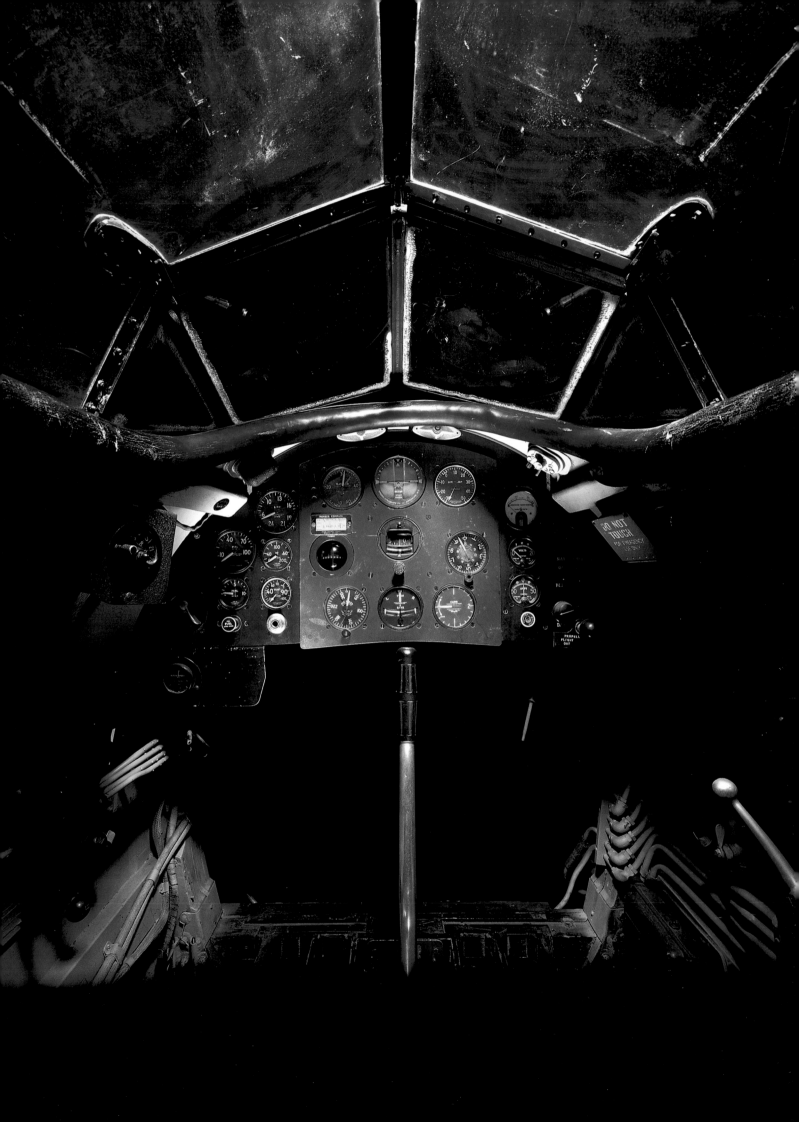

replaced with a new 575-horsepower Wright Cyclone, and its fixed-wheel landing gear replaced with twin Edo floats. The Lindberghs used the reconfigured Sirius to explore the great circle route from Maine to China via Canada, Alaska, Siberia, and Japan. Their journey, in support of Pan American Airways, lasted from July 27 through October 2, ending when the Sirius was damaged at Hankow, China.

In 1933, the Lindberghs flew the repaired Sirius, now mounting a 710-horsepower Cyclone F engine, on a second trip for Pan American, this time exploring transatlantic commercial air routes. From July through December 1933, the Lindberghs surveyed routes through Greenland, Europe (as far east as Moscow), Africa, South America, and the Caribbean. It was on this trip that the Sirius picked up its nickname, *Tingmissartoq*. In Greenland, Anne Lindbergh noticed that local children would call, "*Tingmissartoq!*" whenever her husband took local officials on survey flights. The name translates from Innuit as "one who flies like a big bird."

The Lindberghs flew as a team, seated beneath a sliding canopy in the Sirius's wooden monocoque fuselage. Charles did most of the piloting from his position in the forward cockpit, though Anne was a licensed pilot and could fly the aircraft from the rear cockpit if necessary. Anne handled most of the air-to-ground communications and collected much of the navigational data. With no interphone, their communications with each other took the form of a few words yelled above the engine noise, hand signals, and notes passed between cockpits.

For the Lindberghs, precision navigation was fundamental to the accuracy of every map they prepared, and essential to their survival. Though they flew with the best navigational instruments available, each instrument had limitations. Magnetic compasses could fluctuate widely at the northern latitudes; radio direction finders relied on undependable tube technology and atmospheric conditions to pick up irregular signals from ground stations; sextants, used to take bearings on the sun or stars, were useless in clouds or fog; likewise, drift bearings on parachute flares (which were dropped from the aft cockpit) could be obscured by undercast and fog; even the most reliable instruments, run by gyroscopes, would deviate over time as friction slowed the gyros. The directional gyro became the primary navigational instrument, with other instruments providing correction factors each time the gyros were reset.

The front cockpit shows the main instrument panel, which was mounted on rubber pads to isolate instruments from engine-related vibration. (This pioneering development has since become the industry standard.) The center main panel carried the flight instruments, including the Sperry artificial horizon and directional gyro added for the 1933 flight. Switches, electrical instruments, and the propeller pitch control were located to the right, and engine instruments to the left. The open area stored much of the equipment and survival gear carried on the flights.

Bowlus-duPont 1-S-2100 Senior Albatross *Falcon*

Although recognized for his work with Ryan Airlines on the *Spirit of St. Louis*, W. Hawley Bowlus is best known for his glider and sailplane designs. As a soaring enthusiast, he taught Charles and Anne Lindbergh to fly sailplanes in 1929. (Both earned their glider licenses in January 1930. Anne's would be one of the first U.S. glider licenses awarded to a woman.)

Influenced by new German sailplane designs, in 1932 Hawley Bowlus built the Bowlus Super Sailplane. In 1933, he set up shop with Richard C. duPont in San Fernando, California, forming the Bowlus-duPont Sailplane Company in 1934. The new company designed the Senior Albatross (essentially a gull-winged version of the Super Sailplane), building four examples before the firm folded in 1936. Reaction to the Senior

Albatross was sensational. The first three aircraft, beautifully crafted with spruce-plywood skin, performed brilliantly. In 1933, duPont flew his Senior Albatross to a new U.S. soaring distance record. In 1934, he would capture the world soaring distance record and the U.S. soaring altitude record.

Impressed by duPont's performance in the sailplane, Warren E. Eaton commissioned Bowlus to build a Senior Albatross sheathed in mahogany plywood for his use. Eaton christened it *Falcon*. In September 1934, Eaton flew the *Falcon* to a new U.S. soaring altitude record. Following Eaton's death that December, the *Falcon* was donated to the Smithsonian.

The cockpit of the Senior Albatross seemed more sculpted than built. The pilot was comfortable, if

Warren E. Eaton at the controls of his elegant Bowlus-duPont Senior Albatross Falcon in 1934.

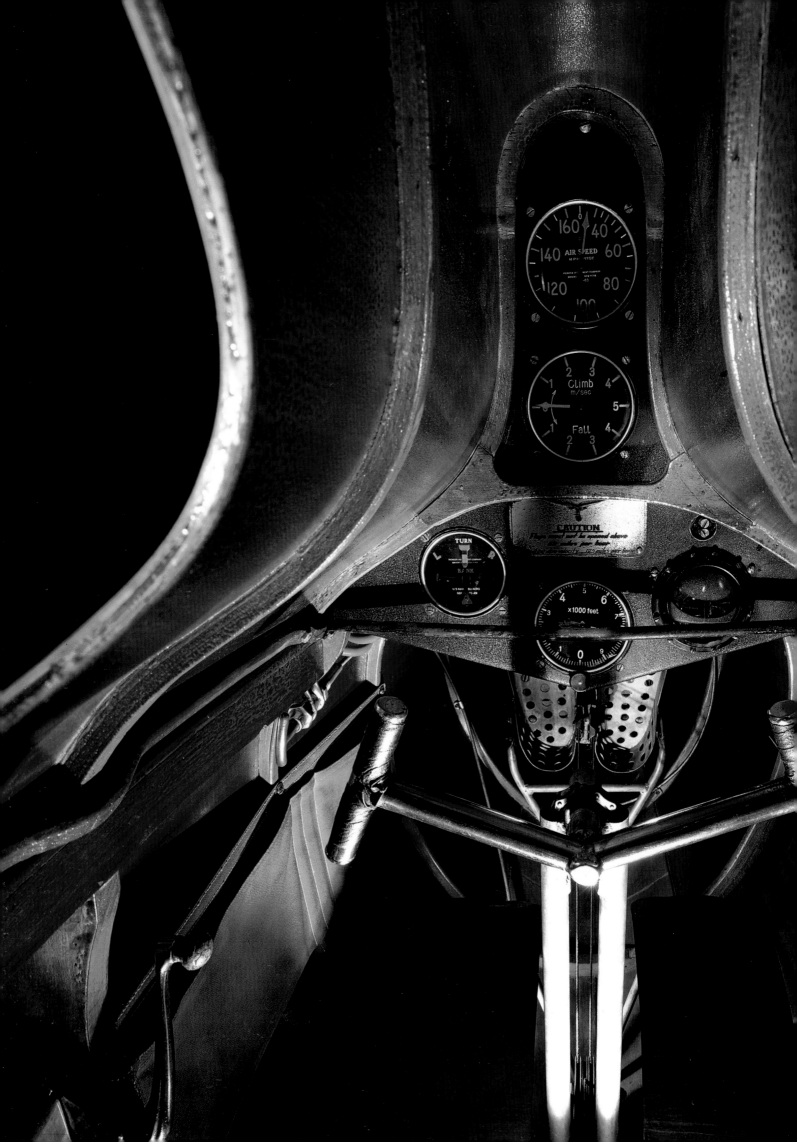

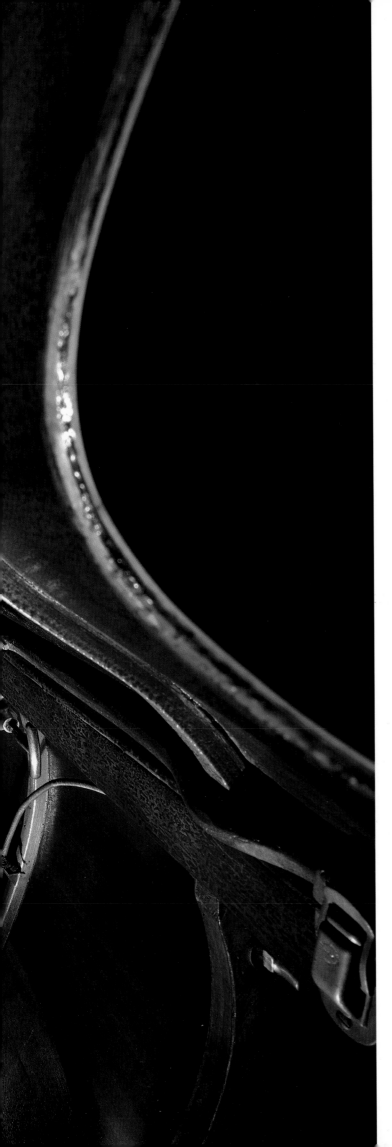

somewhat confined. Wooden rests supported the upper legs, a backpack parachute braced the spine, and metal rudder pedals held the feet. With little room for a conventional rudder bar, the rudder pedals instead pivoted at the pilot's instep: toe pressure turned the rudder. There was also little room for lateral control stick movement, so the ailerons and fully balanced elevators were manipulated by "Dep" controls. A wooden cover latched over the cockpit, further confining the pilot and restricting visibility to a pair of unglazed cutouts at either side. The Senior Albatross carried split trailing-edge flaps, the first ever mounted on an American-built sailplane. These flaps were operated by a lever to the pilot's left.

As an unpowered sailplane, the Senior Albatross needed no instruments for monitoring an engine or electrical system. Still, the panel was advanced for a 1930s sailplane: an airspeed indicator and variometer (rate of climb indicator) were positioned vertically at eye level, with a turn and bank indicator, altimeter, and compass mounted below. (While it may seem remarkable, in light of the Senior Albatross's many long-distance flights, that the only mounted navigational instrument was a compass, it must be remembered that there was no power source to run other instruments.) Two controls were mounted beneath the instrument panel: pulling the right handle released the tow cable, while pulling the left handle activated a brake for the single landing wheel. A final control, mounted to the pilot's right, deployed and retracted the underwing airspeed venturi sensor for the turn and bank indicator.

Boeing P-26A Peashooter

The Boeing P-26A Peashooter is unique in the annals of U.S. Army pursuit aircraft and serves as an excellent example of aviation technology's transition from the wood-and-fabric biplanes of World War I to the all-metal monoplanes of World War II. As such, it is notable as both a first and a last. It was the last Army pursuit plane to have an open cockpit, fixed landing gear, and externally braced wings. At the same time, it was also the first U.S pursuit monoplane and the first all-metal fighter. It began in 1931 as a joint project between Boeing and the U.S. Army, with Boeing building the airframe and the Army providing the engine, propeller, instruments, and armament. The first P-26 was completed at Boeing Field and flown on March 20, 1932. The first P-26A flight was on December 7, 1933.

The P-26 was well received when it entered the U.S. Army Air Corps inventory in 1934. The pilots were immediately impressed with its many advanced characteristics. General Ira Eaker would later remember, "It was its maneuverability, loop, roll, climb, and dive capability which impressed us most." High praise for the new fighter that for a short time was the fastest fighter in service. However, aeronautical progress was rapid in the 1930s, and the Peashooter enjoyed only a relatively brief

An Army Air Corps P-26A in flight over Louisiana in the mid-1930s.

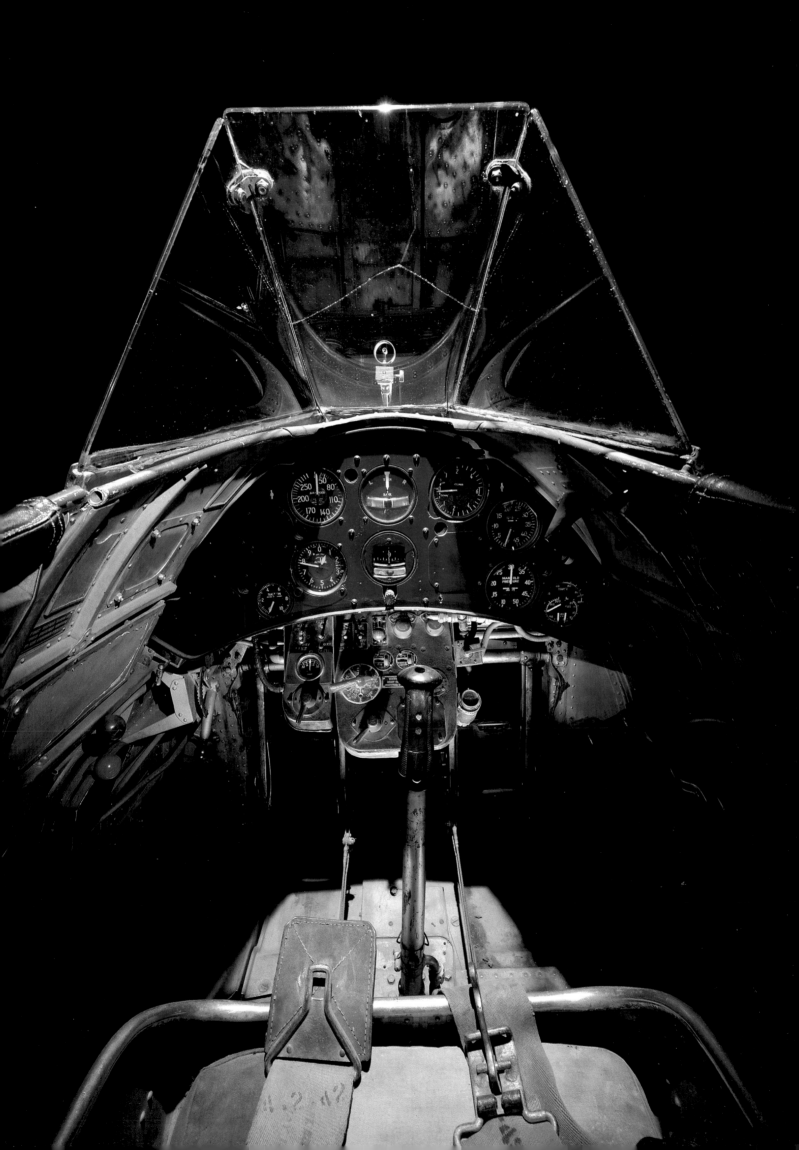

moment of glory. By the time the Japanese attacked Pearl Harbor, just eight years after the P-26A's first flight, only a handful remained in service.

When the Peashooter was removed from regular service, those aircraft stationed overseas were sold to the host countries. Twelve Peashooters were sold to the Philippine Air Force in July 1941. During a Japanese attack on the Philippines, on December 10, 1941, six of the Peashooters were used to counterattack the invaders. Though woefully outclassed performance-wise, they managed to score victories over several of the faster, more modern Japanese aircraft.

Eleven P-26As were sold to China and one to Spain. Those serving in the Philippines and China fought gallantly against the invading Japanese, scoring numerous successes before their destruction by the more numerous and more modern aircraft of their adversaries. Many of the Panamanian Peashooters were later resold to the Guatemalan Air Force. Some of these flew until the early 1950s.

The NASM P-26A was one of the Peashooters sold to Guatemala in 1942. It served until 1954 and was donated to the Smithsonian Institution by the government of Guatemala in 1957. It was loaned to, and restored by, the U.S. Air Force Museum, then returned in 1975 to be displayed in the new National Air and Space Museum.

The standard P-26A cockpit was relatively Spartan, even by contemporary standards. While the NASM Peashooter displays many of its original instrument types, the instrument panel has been modified at some time during its life, most likely during its service in Guatemala. The modification allowed more instruments to be mounted in the panel, while moving the original ones to different positions. Additionally, the original instruments were recessed and had individual lighting, as opposed to the flush-mounted instruments present today. For example, the positions of the turn and bank indicator and the magnetic compass seen in the center of the photograph have been reversed. In the original panel the compass was on top of the turn and bank. The vertical velocity indicator, seen just to the right of the turn and bank, was not a part of the original panel. The original instrument panel ended just to the left of the present airspeed indicator (which appears to be original) and altimeter (which is not original). The small auxiliary sub-panel, located just below the compass in the photo, is original and in the correct location. It provides control of the fuel management system, lighting, and weapons. The smaller sub-panel just to the left was previously positioned to the left of the original instrument panel, above and to the left of where it is now located. It contains the ignition switch and electrical system switch and gauge, and appears to have been moved to accommodate four new instruments when the panel was modified.

Northrop Gamma 2B *Polar Star*

By the time John K. "Jack" Northrop formed his own aircraft company in 1927, he had already established his reputation as an aircraft designer. His new company soon produced a revolutionary line of all-metal monoplanes, starting with the Alphas and the Betas. In January 1932, Northrop set up the Northrop Corporation, a partially owned subsidiary of Douglas Aircraft Co. The new company continued to develop Northrop's aluminum monoplanes, designing the Deltas and the Gammas. The first two aircraft delivered that year were Gammas, the second of which, the Gamma 2B, was delivered to polar explorer Lincoln Ellsworth. Ellsworth named the aircraft the *Polar Star*.

In 1933, Ellsworth formed an Antarctic expedition and left for New Zealand by ship. The expedition arrived in Antarctica in January 1934, planning to fly the *Polar Star* across the mostly unexplored continent. Weather, accidents, engine problems, and personality clashes plagued the explorers, and it would be November 1935 before a reformed expedition team would attempt the transpolar flight. On November 23, Ellsworth and Canadian pilot Herbert Hollick-Kenyon took off from Dundee Island and headed across Antarctica to Little America. The pair were forced to land four times during their journey and were weathered in for days at a time. On December 5, fuel exhaustion forced them down

The Polar Star *carried enough food and equipment to sustain Ellsworth and Hollick-Kenyon during their two-month journey across the Antarctic wastelands.*

about 25 miles (40 km) short of their goal. They walked for six days to reach the camp abandoned by Richard E. Byrd several years earlier. On January 15, 1936, the British Research Society ship *Discovery II* sighted the explorers, who had been missing for nearly two months. Hollick-Kenyon soon recovered the *Polar Star*, which Ellsworth donated to the Smithsonian in April 1936.

The bright yellow-green of the *Polar Star*'s cockpit came from a tinted zinc-chromate anti-corrosive primer used on all interior aluminum surfaces. Forward of the cockpits, most of the fuselage was an open storage compartment; a radiating wire screen kept cargo and equipment from shifting aft to interfere with the pilot's controls. Flight controls were the familiar stick and rudder pedals. (The aft cockpit originally carried a second set of controls, which were removed before the aircraft was donated to the Smithsonian.) A crank to the left of the pilot's seat trimmed pitch and roll; in one mode, the crank adjusted the horizontal stabilizer angle of incidence, while the other mode trimmed the aileron positions. The rudder trim control was to the pilot's right, attached to the back of the radio receiver control panel. Two separate quadrants to the pilot's left controlled the engine and propeller: the forward quadrant held throttle and mixture controls, while the aft quadrant (not seen in our photo) included the propeller pitch and carburetor heat control. Above the throttle, a handle opened the engine shutters to control the temperature of the air-cooled engine. (Hidden above the shutter handle, a jack appears to have provided power for the pilot's electrically heated flight suit.)

The main instrument panel held most of the flight and directional instruments, with engine instruments to the left, flight instruments at the center, and fuel and temperature gauges to the right. The aft cockpit held a chart table and several navigational instruments, including a massive Pioneer Star C Straight Flight Compass, an airspeed indicator, an altimeter, and a drift sight. A hand-held sextant was especially important, since magnetic readings were often inaccurate near the poles.

The radio transmitter control unit was centered beneath the instrument panel, with a hand-cranked trailing wire antenna beneath the fuel-tank selector switches. The radio receiver control was to the pilot's right just aft of the main instrument panel. Both devices failed on the transantarctic flight.

Hughes Special 1B Racer

In 1934, Howard Hughes, Richard Palmer, and Glenn Odekirk designed the Hughes Special 1B Racer (popularly known as the H-1) to be world's the fastest land plane. On Friday, September 13, 1935, Hughes achieved that goal by flying the 1B to a record 567.155 kilometers per hour (approximately 352 mph) over a specially instrumented three-kilometer course near Santa Ana, California. Making one last run over the course, Hughes exhausted his fuel supply, and unable to lower the main landing gear, he brought the aircraft in for a controlled wheels-up landing.

Since the 1B suffered only minor damage, Hughes, Palmer, and Odekirk decided to rebuild it with longer wings and additional fuel capacity for an attempt on the transcontinental speed record. (Despite these and other modifications, the racer retained its original "1B" designation in all of Howard Hughes's records.) At 2:14 A.M. (Pacific Standard Time) on January 19, 1937, Hughes departed Los Angeles, and at just after noon (Eastern Standard Time) he landed at Newark Airport, just outside New York City, setting a new transcontinental record time of 7 hours, 28 minutes, and 25 seconds. It would

Howard Hughes's Special 1B Racer, photographed in California in 1945.

be Hughes's last flight in the 1B, though the aircraft was flown by several others through the 1940s. However, when Hughes donated the racer to the new National Air and Space Museum in 1975, the aircraft had only 40 hours of flight time.

At first sight, the 1B's cockpit is a jumble of hoses, cables, and bicycle chains, instruments, handles, cranks, and switches. The canopy is split down a center seam, with the two halves sliding into the cockpit sides. A crank to the right of the seat (aft of the view in our photo) slid the windscreen forward, improving access. Beside the crank, a lever raised the seat to improve the pilot's view over the nose during takeoffs and landings.

Flight controls were the conventional stick and rudder pedals, with bungee adjustments to help trim the aircraft and lessen pilot fatigue. The rudder bungee knob was centered beneath the instrument panel. The similar aileron bungee knob was just outboard of the pilot's left knee, and just aft a black-handled crank drove the bicycle chain of the elevator bungee. The throttle and mixture control were mounted on the left. The 1B's main landing gear was retracted hydraulically, with a control lever on the floor to the right of the seat. In the event of hydraulic failure, a pipe handle over the gear switch manually pumped the system, or a red cruciform knob to the right of the pump used engine oil pressure to lower the wheels. Pulling the wooden handle at the right of the instrument panel activated the hydraulic brakes on both wheels. The tail skid was retracted by a mechanical, chain-driven crank (seen at the lower left of the photo). A similar crank on the right side lowered the flaps and dropped the ailerons 15 degrees to improve lift along the full length of the wing during takeoffs and landings. Just above, a smaller crank adjusted the propeller pitch. Hand holds above the prop pitch crank and throttles were covered in leather to protect the pilot's knuckles.

Two leather-covered handles centered over the instrument panel opened the access hatches to the Hughes Racer's fuselage and wing fuel tanks. Tank selector switches were beside the pilot's left leg. Just forward of the seat, a floor switch was installed to control the auxiliary wing tanks that were added prior to the transcontinental flight. A wobble pump (not seen in our photo) was mounted on the floor to the left of the seat. The 1B had no fuel gauges. Fuel ran from the tanks through clear (now yellowed) plastic tubing under and around the instrument panel. This system told the pilot if each tank was dry, but otherwise gave no indications of remaining fuel.

The 1B's instrument panel was revised and upgraded several times before its first flight, but the most dramatic changes came before the transcontinental flight. For long-range navigation, the center of the panel was cut away and replaced with a Sperry gyro compass and artificial horizon, linked to a Sperry autopilot. A radio was mounted behind the seat, and a pilot's oxygen system was added. A small electrical light switch panel (seen just aft of the throttle quadrant) may not have been present when Hughes flew the aircraft; no instrument illumination or navigation/landing lights were supposed to have been rigged before the night takeoff on his transcontinental flight. An autopilot switch is located on the floor to the right of the seat, but this may also have been a later addition.

Grumman G-22 *Gulfhawk II*

The single Grumman G-22 was an aerobatic demonstration aircraft built for the Gulf Oil Companies. Based on Grumman's F2F and F3F naval fighters, the G-22 was delivered to the head of Gulf's aviation department, Major Alfred "Al" Williams, in December 1936. Williams would use the aircraft, which he named *Gulfhawk II*, to thrill air show spectators throughout the U.S. and Europe until 1948 (when the aircraft was donated to the Smithsonian). During World War II, the aircraft supported the war effort by testing fuels and lubricants under extreme operating conditions, and by demonstrating airmanship and precision aerobatic flying to military pilot trainees.

The *Gulfhawk II* drew much of its cockpit layout from its Navy fighter forebears. The standard sliding canopy closed behind the unarmored windscreen. The adjustable seat was recessed for the pilot's seat-pack parachute. Flight controls were also standard, though the

The Gulfhawk II *wore Gulf Oil's bright orange, with black, white and blue trim.*

stick had no gun trigger. Mounted to the left were the throttle and mixture control, a knurled wheel for regulating oil temperatures, rudder and stabilizer trim wheels, the tail-wheel lock, the underwing landing-light retraction lever, and a bomb release! (Williams pioneered the art of dive bombing, often dropping inert bombs as part of his air show demonstrations.)

To the right side, thirty turns of a hand-crank retracted or lowered the landing gear, while just forward a sliding arrow marked the gear's position. And should the pilot attempt a landing without lowering his gear, a large red light illuminated if the engine speed dropped below 1200 rpm while the gear was still retracted.

The cockpit configuration was personalized by Williams, who directed Grumman to alter much of the layout to match the cockpit of his earlier Curtiss *Gulfhawk IA*, while adding updated instruments and controls. He relocated the breech of the Coffman cartridge-type engine starter to the cockpit, allowing engine starts without help from the ground crew. Thirty cartridges were boxed just to the left of the control stick.

The crinkle-finished center of the main panel was fully equipped for instrument flying. It included Pioneer airspeed, rate of climb, and turn and bank indicators, a Kollsman altimeter, and a Sperry gyro-horizon and directional gyro. The *Gulfhawk II's* airframe was designed to withstand the high stresses imposed by aerobatics. Williams installed a Pioneer accelerometer just below the main panel, allowing him to monitor his most severe aerobatic maneuvers without overstressing the aircraft. (This practice has since become standard for aerobatic pilots.) Williams also installed a gravity tank to fuel the engine during long periods of inverted flight (with a switch seen forward and right of the control stick), a configuration reminiscent of Domenjoz's Blériot XI twenty years earlier.

As a flying test bed, the *Gulfhawk II* was well equipped to monitor most aspects of engine operation. To the left of the main panel, above the red-and-black-handled fuel wobble pump, twin gauges measured oil inlet and outlet temperatures. Just above sat the fuel-flow gauge, and to the left, an oil-pressure gauge. A second oil-pressure gauge was to the right of the main panel (mounted in the clock's original position), above the engine manifold pressure gauge, tachometer, and carburetor temperature gauge. The carburetor heat control was mounted just inside, on the console. Below the throttle quadrant, the exhaust gas analyzer, required with all Wright R-1820 Cyclone engines, provided data necessary to properly control the carburetor fuel-air mixture. And beneath this, a selector and gauge allowed Williams to check the head temperature of each of his nine engine cylinders.

Grumman G-21 Goose

The Grumman G-21 Goose amphibian was designed as a private commuter transport for wealthy executives. The deep fuselage served also as a hull, with room inside for a flight crew of two and six passengers. Customers looking for extra comfort could order such conveniences as a galley and a lavatory. The Goose had a top speed of 180 miles per hour (290 km/h) and range of 800 miles (1,300 km), putting it on a level with many contemporary airliners. It soon drew the attention of the military and commercial operators, who would quickly become Grumman's greatest customers for the G-21. When production ended in 1945, 345 "Gooses" had been built. Many are still in service, some rebuilt with turboprop engines.

A privately owned Grumman G-21A Goose in flight.

The National Air and Space Museum's Goose was built as a G-21A in 1938 and delivered to Asiatic Petroleum Company. When it retired from service in 1982, it had served with several private owners and airlines. It has been restored to resemble one of the early executive transports.

In the cockpit, the pilot flew from the left seat, assisted by a copilot to the right. As was typical in many aircraft of the era, the pilot did most of the flying, with the copilot available to relieve or to assist in emergencies. It was also the copilot's job to crawl through a hatch to the forward section of the hull to help with docking. A second hatch atop the forward fuselage accessed the nose cleat for tying off at the pier.

Some creative design was necessary in arranging instruments and controls around the hatch that bisected the bulkhead in front of the pilots. The main instrument panel became known as the "cathedral" panel because of the center arch over the hatch. The wing-flap switch and most engine-related instruments and controls were located in an overhead console panel between the pilots and directly beneath the twin engines. Gauges for fuel, oil and manifold pressures and oil, cylinder head and carburetor air temperatures were centered on the console, along with the tachometers. The throttles, starter switches, and mixture, flap, prop pitch, and carburetor heat controls were offset to the left, within comfortable reach of the pilot but a bit of a stretch for a short copilot.

The apportioning of other controls and instruments reflected the pilots' differing duties. The altimeter, magnetic compass and chronometer were centered over the cathedral arch, where both could see them. All blind flying instruments and radio controls (including the radio compass) were in the pilot's panel, while the copilot's panel held the fire extinguisher controls, the vacuum source selector switch and suction gauge, and electrical system switches.

Each of the pilots had a control wheel and rudder pedals (with the copilot's rudder pedals folded down in our photo). The rudder-trim control was on the left side wall, accessible only from the left seat, while the elevator trim was to the right of the pilot's seat, in easy reach of both crew members. The manual landing-gear retraction crank was also between the pilots' seats. Either pilot could turn the crank forty-one revolutions to retract or extend the gear.

Northrop N-1M Jeep

In 1939, John K. "Jack" Northrop formed a new aircraft company, Northrop Aircraft, Inc. As a logical extension of Northrop's lifelong interest in aerodynamically clean aircraft, the new company would immediately begin the development of a true flying wing aircraft — an aircraft without the weight and drag of a fuselage, tail, or engine nacelles. The first of these designs, the N-1M (Northrop Model 1 Mockup) Jeep, emerged in July 1940 as a boomerang-shaped prototype built of wood and tubular steel.

The N-1M was a flying aerodynamic test bed, designed to be easily reconfigured as engineers searched for improved stability, control, and performance. Although overweight and chronically underpowered, the Jeep showed enough promise to encourage the development of the improved N-9M and the post-war B-35 and all-jet B-49 flying wing bombers. The N-1M was given to the Smithsonian's National Air Museum in 1946. This aircraft was restored over a four-year period beginning in 1979.

Northrop's N-1M, photographed following its 1983 NASM restoration. The aircraft's twin 120-horsepower, six-cylinder, air-cooled Franklin engines were in the fuselage to either side of the cockpit.

The Jeep's cockpit was small and crowded, and pilot visibility was poor. To improve the latter, the seat was raised several inches. A hole was cut through the sliding canopy to accommodate the pilot's head, with a domed metal cover resealing the hole. (Note that the aircraft's yellow forward decking reflects in the windscreen in our photo; the windscreen itself is unobstructed.) Exiting the cockpit in any emergency would have been difficult and, if the props were turning, dangerous.

The Jeep's familiar flight controls operated an innovative arrangement of control surfaces. The elevators and ailerons were combined as "elevons" on the wing's trailing edge. Pulling or pushing the control column moved the elevons in unison, affecting the aircraft's pitch. Turning the control wheel staggered the elevons, creating roll. The Jeep, of course, had no tail or rudder, but the "rudder" pedals still controlled yaw through split flaps, or "clamshells," which opened at either wing tip. The split flaps could also be opened to increase the glide angle or act as air brakes to reduce airspeed.

The throttle quadrant and mixture controls were in easy reach on the right side of the cockpit. The temporary masking-tape labels were practical expedients befitting the Jeep's status as a prototype. Magneto switches were just forward, and carburetor heat controls (not seen in our view) just aft. Switches along the right-side floor selected fuel tanks and landing gear and flap positions, with a long handle for the wobble pump. An elevon pitch-trim crank was placed over the pilot's right shoulder.

The left side of the cockpit, blocked by fore-and-aft movement of the heavy flight-control column, was relatively empty. A hand pump for the hydraulic system was on the floor beside the seat, and a hand-held fire extinguisher (not seen in our photo) was under the canopy coaming.

The engine fire-extinguisher switch was forward, to the left side of the instrument panel — a difficult reach past the control column, but fortunately never needed.

The instrument panel was simple, with most gauges monitoring the engine. Flight instruments included an altimeter, airspeed indicator, and turn and bank indicator. A floor-mounted gauge for the hydraulic system was removed before the aircraft came to the Museum. It appears that no radio was ever installed.

Kellett XO-60 Autogiro

Although the autogiro — an aircraft that derived its lift from a free-turning rotor — intrigued world military organizations throughout the 1930s, very few of these aircraft saw service during World War II. The autogiro's near vertical takeoff and landing capabilities suggested many possible military applications, but these prospects diminished in the mid-1940s with the development of the helicopter.

The U.S. Army ordered its first developmental autogyro, the YG-1, from the Kellett Autogiro Corporation in 1935. The concept developed until the Army Air Forces ordered seven unarmed two-seat O-60 observation models in 1942. The first six YO-60 developmental airframes were delivered in 1943. The seventh, an experimental prototype designated XO-60, was delivered to Wright Field, Ohio, in December 1944. Now part of the NASM collection, it would be the last autogyro ever delivered to U.S. Army Air Forces.

The XO-60's cockpit was open and roomy. Despite having the narrow rotor mast directly ahead of the windscreen, pilots found forward visibility to be acceptable. The clear sliding canopy was undercut to the fuselage side, granting an excellent downward view supplemented by windows between the pilot's and observer's feet. The pilot sat between the two 18-gallon (68 L) fuel tanks, with the fuel-tank selector switch and red-handled emergency hand-pump (wobble pump) located at his left knee.

The instrument panel was split by the welded steel fuselage structure, with the electrical panel to the left, yellow-outlined blind flying panel to the upper right, and engine and rotor panel to the lower right. The pilot's identification light switches and radio controls were mounted at his right elbow.

One of the AAF's six YO-60s, photographed at Wright Field, Ohio, in 1943. Note the exposed diagonal driveshaft leading from the rear of the engine to the base of the rotor head.

The standard flight controls performed the usual functions, though with a twist. Cables connected the rudder pedals to the rudder, but there were no elevators or ailerons to connect to the main control stick. Instead, all stick motion was translated to the tilting rotor head to alter the XO-60's pitch and roll. Stick forces were reduced by a ratchet longitudinal bungee lever at the pilot's right knee and a lateral bungee knob at his right hip.

Three switches located beneath the electrical panel managed the rotor revolutions and pitch. Although forward motion of the aircraft turned the rotor in flight, power could be diverted from the XO-60's engine to start the rotor on the ground. With the control stick locked forward, preventing stick movement from twisting the rotor head, a small green handle just left of the centerline engaged the rotor gearshift. Farther to the left was the clutch brake, a longer green lever. When pushed forward, the brake locked the rotor, preventing damage during taxiing. The flight manual instructed pilots to first check for any obstructions near the rotor, next "in a stentorian voice call, 'Starting Rotor — CLEAR,'" then slowly pull the clutch lever back while increasing the engine power, gradually increasing the engine rpms. With the rotor up to speed, the pilot could release the control stick and begin a short takeoff run or attempt a "standing jump takeoff." Upon disengaging the red cylindrical safety knob, the pilot forced the long red pitch-control handle forward. This automatically uncoupled the clutch brake and gear and increased the rotor pitch as the XO-60 leapt into the air.

Vought OS2U-3 Kingfisher

Each of the world's fleets developed its own ship-launched observation-scout aircraft between the two world wars. Launched by catapults from battleships and cruisers, these float-equipped aircraft spotted land- and sea-based targets and plotted fire for the ships' big guns before landing in the water to be hoisted back aboard. Although ship-based radar took over many "gun-laying" duties, and enemy fighters and anti-aircraft increased the hazards for any lightly armed, low-powered planes, observation-scout aircraft continued to prove their worth through the end of World War II and beyond.

During the War, the two-seat Vought OS2U Kingfisher served as the U.S. Navy's primary observation-scout type, adding missions for anti-submarine warfare, aircrew training, rescue and general utility. Designed in 1937, the Kingfisher ended production in 1942, with a total of 1,519 built. The Museum's example is an OS2U-3, distinguished from the earlier OS2U-2 by its increased armor for the crew, its increased fuel capacity, and its self-sealing fuel tanks. The aircraft served in the Pacific aboard the battleship USS *Indiana*, and in 1944, its pilot won a Navy Cross for a rescue under fire.

Since a high perch atop a catapult was not easily accessible to deck crews, the Kingfisher replaced the standard Navy hand-cranked inertial starter with a cartridge starter (similar to the *Gulfhawk II*'s). The starter was located just below the instrument panel, over the box of cartridges. Before launch, the pilot latched a spring-loaded clip (seen at the edge of the canopy rail) over the open throttle and grasped a handle over the

Five OS2U-3s assigned to the U.S. Coast Guard at Elizabeth City, North Carolina, in early 1943. Land-based Kingfishers could attach wheeled beaching gear, as seen here, or replace their floats with wheeled landing gear.

coaming with his left hand. (Without this precaution, the acceleration of a catapult launch could jerk the pilot's throttle hand aft, cutting engine power at a dangerous time.) The flap handle, located beneath the throttle quadrant, lowered wing flaps and depressed ailerons, generating extra lift along the wing's entire trailing edge. Once ready, the pilot signaled, and the deck crew fired the aircraft off the cat.

Open-sea landings could be difficult in an aircraft as light as the Kingfisher. Whenever possible, the floatplane landed parallel to, and leeward of, its ship, a position that offered some protection from wind and waves. The pilot then taxied onto a towed recovery sled, the observer attached a cable from the ship to a fitting behind the pilot's seat, and the aircraft was raised to the deck by ship's crane.

Although the Kingfisher was not primarily an offensive weapon, it was armed nonetheless. An ammunition box centered under the instrument panel held belted 30-caliber rounds for the single fixed machine gun. Holes punched in the box showed how many bullets remained. The gun itself (not mounted in the Museum's Kingfisher) was attached to brackets beneath the instrument panel, to the right of the ammo box. A chute beneath collected spent rounds and links. For defensive purposes, the observer had a second 30-caliber gun on a flexible mount in the aft cockpit. Underwing racks allowed the Kingfisher to carry two 100-pound (45 kg) bombs or two 325-pound (147 kg) depth charges. Kingfishers carrying depth charges were credited with sinking two U-boats during anti-submarine patrols in 1942.

Grumman F4F-4 (FM-1) Wildcat

The Grumman F4F Wildcat was the primary U.S. Navy and Marine Corps fighter when the U.S. entered World War II. A monoplane, its development from Grumman's earlier F3F biplane fighter began in 1936. The first production variant was the F4F-3. Delivered in early 1940, it carried two machine guns in each wing. During the first few months of the War, the Wildcat proved capable against Japanese bombers, but seriously deficient against Japan's nimble, lightweight fighters.

By the Battle of Midway in June 1942, most U.S. Navy fighter squadrons were reequipping with the new F4F-4 version of the Wildcat. The "Dash 4" featured folding wings (allowing more aircraft to be stored on a carrier flight deck) and an additional heavy machine gun in each wing. As both features increased the Wildcat's weight and reduced the ammo capacity, the new variant proved unpopular with many pilots.

Having pushed the Wildcat design to its limits, Grumman turned to the design and production of a new fighter, the F6F Hellcat. To keep up with its growing need for fighters, the Navy ordered more Wildcats, transferring the production to General Motors' Eastern Aircraft Division. Now designated FM-1, General Motors' Wildcats were essentially F4F-4s with the wing armament reduced to four machine guns. NASM's Wildcat is an FM-1, restored by Grumman to represent an F4F-4.

The Wildcat cockpit developed from the F3F cockpit and shared many features with Al Williams's G-22 *Gulfhawk II*, most notably the hand-cranked landing-gear

A flight of four General Motors-built FM-1 Wildcats from a U.S. Navy escort carrier, photographed in mid-1943.

retraction mechanism at the right of the cockpit. The Navy pilot soon learned to tighten his throttle for take-off. If he needed to hold the throttle with his left hand while turning the crank with his right, he could steady the control stick only with his knees. (The novice pilot's takeoff often featured a distinctive wobble; in the confined cockpit, his knees would move every time he turned the crank!)

To land on aircraft carriers, the Wildcat was equipped with a tail hook, controlled by the yellow-and-black handle at the front of the left canopy rail. Since the wings were folded manually by the deck crew, no wing-fold switches, locks, or indicators were present in the Wildcat cockpit.

The instrument panel arrangement was nearly identical for the F4F-4 and the FM-1 (though Grumman performed a considerable panel rearrangement between the F4F-3 and the F4F-4). The gun sight atop the FM-1 panel was the "Illuminating Sight Mark 8," a U.S. Navy development of the British Mark II sight seen in the Spitfire.

Long overwater flights dictated that Navy fighter pilots be fully capable of navigating to their targets and back to their carriers. A sliding wood and clear plastic chart table (normally stored beneath the instrument panel) gave the Wildcat pilot a flat work surface. (Again, although the aircraft could be trimmed for level flight, the control stick was often steadied by the pilot's knees.) The smooth black and dark green cockpit colors helped reduce glare and reflection on the instruments and chart table, especially when flying at night.

Supermarine Spitfire HF.Mark VII

To its pilots, the Supermarine Spitfire was a near perfect blend of power, maneuverability and beauty. To the British, the Spitfire was the legendary fighter that, along with the Hawker Hurricane, saved their nation during the summer of 1940. Over a period of sixteen weeks, from mid-July through the end of October, the outnumbered "Spits" and "Hurries" of Royal Air Force (RAF) Fighter Command repelled Germany's Luftwaffe in the Battle of Britain.

Between 1936 and 1948, British factories produced over 20,000 Spitfires in dozens of variants. One hundred and forty of them were of the HF. Mark VII high-altitude fighter variant. First produced in 1942, the HF. VII mounted a new Rolls Royce Merlin 71 engine, a four-bladed prop, extended wing tips, and partially pressurized cockpit, all to improve performance at altitudes over 40,000 feet (12,000 m). A two-stage supercharger, which compressed thinner high-altitude air to sustain

The National Air and Space Museum's Spitfire was evaluated by the U.S. Army Air Forces.
It is seen here during a wartime test flight over Ohio in 1943.

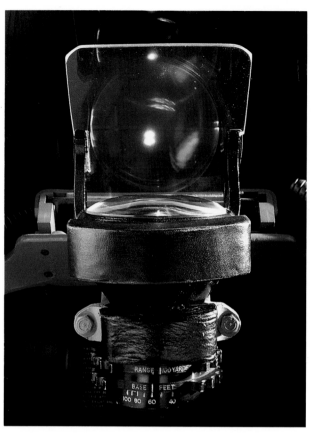

Illuminated reflector gun sights focused on the aiming point in front of the aircraft and compensated for pilot head movement inside the cockpit. The Spitfire's G.M. 2 gun sight was adapted for use in many U.S. fighters.

the engine, slammed into high gear as the aircraft climbed through about 21,000 feet (6,400 m). The crashing noise of the changing gears startled most new pilots; a switch above the two yellow instruments allowed older hands to lock the supercharger at the lower setting until the higher gear was needed.

In common with most contemporary fighter designs, the Spitfire mated the largest possible engine with the smallest possible airframe, leaving little room for the pilot. Shoulder room was so tight that few could comfortably wear the heavy fleece-lined jackets that were then popular in the RAF. Entering the HF. VII was also more difficult than it had been on most earlier marks: to maintain cockpit pressurization, designers had eliminated the convenient access hatch from the cockpit's left side. The sliding canopy was also gone, replaced by a separate pressurized hood that could only be mounted or removed by ground crew. Once this hood was locked in place, pilots used the "direct vision panel" at the left of the windscreen for low-altitude ventilation and visibility. This opening panel was eliminated when a new sliding pressurized canopy was devised for later-production HF. VIIs.

On the HF. VII, the circular bracket to the right of the panel normally mounted a cabin-pressure altimeter;

the two red warning lights at the edge of the bracket came on if cockpit pressure dropped below safe levels.

Spitfire instruments were organized around the RAF "Basic Six." In the late 1930s, the RAF standardized blind flying instruments. The center of each instrument panel would carry (from the left) an airspeed indicator, artificial horizon, and vertical speed (rate of climb) indicator. The second row would carry an altimeter, heading indicator (directional gyro or gyro compass), and turn and bank indicator. For most of the War, this level of standardization was unique to the RAF.

Although the Spitfire control column had full fore-and-aft movement, it was articulated above the pilot's legs for lateral movement (a design response to the lack of leg room). The two-handed spade-grip incorporated the brake lever, machine gun and cannon fire control, and gun camera push-button. Two-position rudder pedals were designed to reduce leg fatigue and give maximum rudder control. Mounted to the left side of the cockpit, the throttle was linked to an "undercarriage warning horn." Because some pilots forgot to lower their landing gear before landing, the horn was set to sound if the throttle closed beyond a certain point while the gear was still retracted. Similar systems remain in use on the vast majority of modern aircraft.

Focke-Wulf Fw 190 F-8

The first engagement between the German Focke-Wulf 190 As and British Spitfire Mk.Vs occurred in August 1941, and both sides immediately recognized the German fighter's superiority. Powered by the BMW 801 series radial engine, the Fw 190 had been designed by Focke-Wulf engineer Kurt Tank to meet a 1937 German Air Ministry (RLM) specification. Tank overcame the inherent drag penalties of the radial by enclosing it behind a twelve-bladed cooling fan inside a tight NACA-style cowl. A very slim fuselage with steeply raked windscreen and faired sliding canopy further reduced drag. The first prototype flew on June 1, 1939.

By 1942, the RLM recognized the need for a fast, durable, and readily available fighter-bomber to support its infantry and armored units in North Africa and Russia. Tank quickly modified a Fw 190 A and received a contract for what would be known as the Fw 190 F series. The Fw 190 was adapted to this new role by installing additional armor protection and two underwing hard points, each holding a 50-kilogram (110 lb) bomb. (The Fw 190 A's outboard machine gun was removed from each wing to compensate for the increased bomb load.) The existing centerline rack could still carry a 300-liter (80 gal) fuel tank, a 250-kilogram (550 lb) bomb, or four 50-kilogram (110 lb) bombs. Entering service in the spring of 1944, the Fw 190 F-8 was the final ground-attack variant produced in large numbers and was used until the War's end. The F-8 featured increased horsepower, new wing hard points to carry heavier loads, lighter armor to increase performance, and an improved visibility canopy. Some examples featured more powerful cannons, ground-attack missiles, and anti-shipping torpedoes.

For Luftwaffe pilots making the transition from the Messerschmitt Bf 109, the Fw 190 cockpit offered distinct advantages in room and visibility. No longer shoehorned into a tight cockpit with a claustrophobic canopy over his head, the Fw 190 pilot found an open

Captured and transferred to the United States in 1945, NASM's F-8 is seen following restoration in 1983. It is the most complete and accurately restored Focke-Wulf Fw 190 in the world.

environment with side consoles and controls that were easy to reach, read, and operate. The windscreen raked forward, unlike the Bf 109's nearly vertical windscreen which loomed dangerously close to the pilot's face. The bubble canopy offered better headroom and nearly 360-degree visibility, elements undreamed of in the Messerschmitts.

Noted for their simplicity and order, German cockpits used letter- and color-coding to allow pilots to quickly identify different systems. NASM's Fw 190 F-8 cockpit was painted in the typical dark gray used to reduce instrument and canopy reflections. The control stick was topped by the gun-firing button. Standard Luftwaffe rudder pedals, with straps to secure the pilot's feet, were mounted behind and below the instrument panel. The instrument panel was split, with all flight instruments to the left of the raised section, and engine instruments to the right and on the recessed section. The round red push/pull button at the left of the lower panel was an emergency engine power boost control, and the red-knobbed lever below it, the fuel-tank selector. Controls on the left console were for the radio, flaps, and landing gear, all electrically operated to save weight and eliminate a combat-vulnerable hydraulic system. The yellow-trimmed throttle lever with thumb-operated electric prop-pitch control was to the left (with changes in engine speed automatically translated into changes in propeller pitch), beneath the canopy rail, and the yellow fuel-primer switch farther aft on the left console. Above the right console, a gray-handled wheel cranked the canopy open and closed; the red-tagged lever behind the wheel jettisoned the canopy. On the right console, from front to rear, are the 24-hour clock mount (the clock is missing), a small red starter button, and a series of five circuit breakers. A map case was mounted below the console, beside the pilot's right knee. The oxygen control unit was on a bulkhead behind the right console. Left and above the upper instrument panel were vertical ammunition counters for the four guns. The body of the Revi gun and bomb sight is visible to the right of the ammo counters, though the gun sight reflector glass above the coaming cannot be seen in this photo.

Ilyushin Il-2M3 Shturmovik

In May 1945, as the final assault on Berlin took place, the Soviet Union possessed the largest tactical air arm in the world. At the core of this air juggernaut was *Shturmovaya aviatsia,* or "ground-attack aviation." And at the core of Soviet ground-attack aviation was Sergei Ilyushin's Il-2 Shturmovik. The Shturmovik was born under the stress of Stalin's dictatorship and raised under the strain of the German invasion of the Soviet Union. Despite this, over 36,000 Shturmoviks were reportedly produced — the highest production figure for any combat aircraft type in history.

Few aircraft types have been so focused on a specific mission or have accomplished their mission so well. One of the primary reasons that the Il-2 was able to accomplish its ground-attack is its *Bronekorpus* (armored shell). Constructed from 5-to-12-millimeter-thick nickel-molybdenum steel alloy, the shell surrounded the most vulnerable and vital parts of the aircraft: the crew, the engine, and the fuel and oil tanks. The Shturmovik was a "winged tank." Its role was to attack the huge German tank columns on the Eastern Front, and it did that extremely well. The Germans referred to the Il-2 as the *Schwarzer Tod* (Black Death).

While the heavily armed (two 23 mm cannons, two 7.62 mm machine guns, four internal bomb bays, and up to eight RS-82 rockets were common) Il-2 enjoyed tremendous success against German tanks, it also suffered an extremely high attrition rate. One Shturmovik was lost for every thirty combat sorties flown, and early in the War, when the Soviets had little or no fighter support, the loss rate was even higher. Most surviving aircraft were scrapped after the War, and today only ten are known to exist.

Noteworthy in the cockpit photo is the lack of a gun sight or bomb-aiming device. The originally installed PBP-1 sight was unpopular with pilots because of the serious head injuries it caused during the frequent crash landings. The replacement, a rudimentary VV-1 sight, used an external sight through the diamond-shaped area of the 49 mm armored-glass windscreen and allowed a protective cushion (visible at the center of the canopy bow) to be installed.

Simple flight instruments are visible in the center panel, while the six engine instruments are on the left. Soviet aircraft of the era were famous for their austere instrumentation. The throttle and mixture control is located on the left, just under the glare shield. On the left console, the inboard lever is the landing-gear control. On the control stick, the switches in the center control the cannons and machine guns, while the bomb (left) and rocket (right) controls are attached on the top. The green canister with the attached lever on the right side panel is the emergency landing-gear control, and just below that, with the yellow-colored tubing, is the fuel control system.

NASM's Il-2 was recovered in the early 1990s from a lake approximately 100 kilometers (62 miles) south of St. Petersburg, Russia. It is now thought to have been one of a group of five Shturmoviks that force-landed on the frozen lake surface in January 1944 after losing their bearings in deteriorating weather, running low on fuel, and finding themselves behind German lines.

The NASM Il-2 was partially restored before being donated to the museum. The cockpit area is complete.

The Museum's Shturmovik, photographed in storage without its outer wing panels attached.

North American Aviation P-51D Mustang

North American Aviation designed the Mustang in 1940 for Britain's Royal Air Force. The aircraft would soon prove itself superior to the Spitfire at altitudes under 20,000 feet (6,000 m), prompting the U.S. Army Air Forces to order several hundred dive-bomber and ground-support versions for their own use. Hoping to improve high-altitude performance, in early 1942 the British first tested a replacement of the Mustang's low-altitude Allison engine with a Rolls Royce Merlin engine. Encouraged by the results, the RAF pressed North American to produce this new version. By August 1942, North American could report to the Army Air Forces, in what had to be one of World War II's great understatements, "If the aerodynamics isn't ruined, looks like they might have a pretty good airplane."

The aerodynamics *weren't* ruined, and the Merlin-equipped Mustang became one of the finest fighters of World War II. The inline engine and laminar flow wings allowed for a very clean design. With additional fuselage and underwing fuel tanks, Mustangs could escort bombers across all of Europe from British or Italian bases, or over the Japanese home islands from bases on Iwo Jima. Fuel management was critical to these long-range missions. By turning the fuel selector switch (see page 78), the pilot would first empty the fuselage tank to move his center of gravity forward. The underwing drop tanks, which carried up to forty-five percent of the Mustang's total fuel capacity, would be next. (Even if partially filled, the drop tanks had to be jettisoned before attempting combat with enemy aircraft.) The drop tanks

Colonel Ward W. Harker, commander of the 54th Fighter Group, at the controls of his P-51D, Bartow Field, Florida, 1944.

would be carefully alternated to prevent the center of gravity from moving too far left or right; the same technique would be used when the wing tanks were selected.

The P-51D version (called "Mustang Mark IV" in the RAF) added a clear-view "bubble" canopy, which gave its pilots 180 degrees of visibility. Forward visibility, of course, was another matter. On the ground, Mustang pilots would often execute a series of S-turns along the taxiway just to be able to see any obstructions ahead. The new canopy had another advantage: using the red-handled emergency canopy release (on the right, just beneath the canopy coaming), the pilot could quickly jettison his canopy for an emergency exit.

The Mustang cockpit was a close fit, but not uncomfortably so for most pilots. Though well heated, the cockpit was unpressurized. On early Allison-equipped aircraft, the pilot's feet rested on the upper surface of the main fuel tank. With the installation of the Merlin, the wing was repositioned several inches lower (a concession to aerodynamics). To fill the space, Merlin-equipped Mustangs carried plywood floors covered with a black non-skid surface.

Instrument panels for the first Mustangs, ordered to RAF specifications, carried a blind flying panel in the same "Basic Six" arrangement as the Spitfire and all other British military aircraft. Although the U.S. had not adopted its own standardized instrument layout, the subsequent Mustangs ordered for the AAF completely revised the blind flying panel. By mid-1943, the AAF was teaching instrument flying with a new standard

panel arrangement. On Mustangs, the P-51D was the first variant to adopt the new layout.*

As with many World War II fighters, the Mustang allowed its pilot to manage most of his critical systems without taking his hands off the throttle (mounted high and forward, on the left) and control stick during combat. The microphone switch was a button at the center of the throttle handle. The K-14 lead-computing gun sight (not installed on the Museum's example) could be adjusted by twisting that handle. Gun triggers were in the customary position on the control stick. Bomb-salvo levers were just ahead of the throttles, but with most Mustangs used as escort fighters, drop tanks were usually carried instead of bombs.

Radio systems for late-war Mustangs often included a new tail-warning radar. Controls for the AN/APS-13 were mounted to the right of the cockpit, with the other communications equipment. The warning light, however, was mounted just above the coaming, to the left of the gun sight, a convenient alarm should any aircraft suddenly approach from behind, and an electric alarm bell was mounted beneath the seat.

*The new U.S. standard blind flying panel comprised six instruments, grouped in the following order: (top row, left to right) airspeed indicator, directional gyro, artificial horizon; (bottom row, left to right) altimeter, turn and bank indicator, rate of climb indicator. Early U.S. Mustangs used a similar arrangement, with the positions of the altimeter and airspeed indicator reversed.

Aichi M6A1 Seiran

Influenced by the Doolittle raid on Tokyo on April 18, 1942, the Imperial Japanese Navy issued specifications to the Aichi Aircraft Co. for a single-engine, float-mounted bomber capable of being transported, launched, and recovered by a submarine. This aircraft and its submersible "aircraft carrier," the 393-foot I-400 Class submarine, were tasked with a strategic mission to attack the Panama Canal, slowing the flow of materials from America to the Pacific battle zone. Development of the Seiran was done in such secrecy that the Allies knew very little about it until after the War was over. Most aircraft developed by the Japanese before and during World War II were well known to the Allies and were given English code names. So little was known about the Seiran, which translates as "Storm Out of a Clear Blue Sky," that it never received an Allied code name.

A large watertight tube measuring 11 feet 6 inches (3.5 m) in diameter and mounted on the right side of the conning tower of the I-400 sub served as the "hangar" for three Seirans. With small-diameter, water-cooled engine (based on the German Daimler-Benz 601 series engines) and using an 11-foot-diameter (3.3 m) propeller, the designers reduced all the parts of the aircraft, including a single bomb or torpedo and its mounting/launch dolly, into a package no bigger in diameter than the arc of the propeller. To achieve this, the wings hydraulically rotated the leading edge down ninety degrees and then folded back against the fuselage. The horizontal and vertical stabilizer tips folded, and the two floats and attaching pylons were stored in separate compartments next to the catapult track. When preparing to launch, each aircraft was rolled out of the "hangar" and raised on its mount.

The Seiran was photographed in May 2001, following its restoration by the Museum staff.

All of the components were unfolded and locked, then the floats and their support pylons were attached by quick-connect/disconnect fittings. Crews trained to launch all three aircraft in thirty minutes from the time the sub surfaced.

Development of the Seiran was very slow. By the end of the War, in August 1945, only twenty-eight Seirans were completed, and fewer were operational. Shortages of materials, a poorly trained, largely unskilled workforce, and frequent bomb attacks impeded Seiran production. By the time two I-400 subs and enough Seirans were completed to train crews and fill the six positions in the sub's "hangars," the War was nearly over and the Panama Canal mission was no longer possible. An attack on the American fleet at Ulithi Atoll was launched but aborted when Japan surrendered on August 14, 1945. Both subs scuttled their aircraft, ammunition, and documents before surrendering to the U.S. Navy.

The Seiran cockpit accommodated a crew of two. A pilot, in front, had a complete array of instruments. All engine management, oxygen, flight control, and aiming devices were plainly labeled and easy to reach. The pilot had a height-adjustable seat and rudder pedals, an adjustable cockpit heater, and an ultraviolet light for night instrument and map reading. A fire-suppression system was activated by controls on the lower left corner of the instrument panel. Directly above the instrument panel was the pilot's reflector bomb sight. Notably missing are forward firing guns.

The second crewman acted as navigator, radio operator, and rear gunner. His seat was also height-adjustable and rotated 360 degrees. Facing forward, he viewed a rudimentary instrument panel, above which sat his compasses and radio loop antenna. Trays below the instrument panel held his radio equipment. On the floor to his left was a port for a drift sight to note deviations in the flight direction while over water. In the event of a rear attack, he would swivel his seat aft, permitting him to use a single 13 mm machine gun fed by a 300-round belt.

The NASM Aichi Seiran, the last one produced and the only one still in existence, was returned to the U.S. in 1945 for inspection and transferred to the Smithsonian Institution in 1960. Its restoration was completed in 2000.

Messerschmitt Me 262 A-1a Schwalbe

In June 1944, Germany's Me 262 Schwalbe (Swallow) became the world's first operational jet fighter. (Although the He 280 flew under jet power in April 1941, fifteen months before the 262, the Heinkel fighter never proceeded beyond its test program.) The Me 262's wartime gestation was slow: twenty-one months elapsed between the first jet flight and the April 1944 delivery of the first production examples. At altitude, nothing could catch the 262. In an early speed test, one of the jets topped 624 mph (1,004 km/h), a full 150 mph (240 km/h) faster than any operational Allied fighter. Production aircraft averaged a still-respectable 540 mph (865 km/h). But with its range limited by high fuel consumption, the Me 262 became an easy target for Allied fighters marauding over German airfields. Although 1,443 Me 262s were produced, only about 300 appear to have seen combat, and the fighter's final impact on the outcome of the War was negligible.

NASM's aircraft served with Jagdgeschwader 7 (Fighter Wing 7) and was captured at the War's end at Lechfeld, Germany (a principal Luftwaffe experimental and training base). The aircraft was transported to the United States and test flown briefly at Wright Field, Ohio. It was brought to the Smithsonian's Silver Hill facility in 1950 and restored from 1977 to 1979.

For all its sophistication as an aircraft, the Me 262 showed few advances in its cockpit. Visibility was good, with a 360-degree canopy that had few obstructions. The center canopy section hinged to the right for normal access, but in an emergency was easily jettisoned using the red handle on the forward right canopy rail. Tricycle landing gear and a low nose profile gave the pilot a good view of the runway during takeoffs and landings. The standard Luftwaffe Revi 16B reflecting gun sight could be folded down to the right for an even better forward view. There was a windscreen heater (with its switch at the forward end of the right-hand console) but no cabin heat; a jack was provided for the pilot's electrically heated flight suit.

The twin yellow-handled throttles at the left of the cockpit had push-button engine starters centered in the knobs. Pilots soon learned to be careful when adjusting the throttles: opening them too quickly could cause engine fires, and closing them too quickly could cause a compressor stall and flame out. The yellow-banded red levers beneath the throttles selected fuel tanks, while the single red knob forward of the throttles trimmed the stabilizer. The right console held radio equipment, with a recognition-flare launch panel, electrical circuit breakers, and (in the shadows) a red-handled bomb-drop/tank-jettison handle.

The main instrument panel paired color-coded engine instruments, to the right, with the blind flying panel, to the left. Interestingly, the 262's blind-flying panel is nearly identical to the British Basic Six panel: on the 262 the turn and bank indicator is incorporated in the artificial horizon, leaving the lower right position for the AFN-2 radio homing indicator. A blanked-off position beneath the blind-flying panel was originally planned to hold the cabin pressure gauge, an unnecessary instrument since the 262's cockpit was unpressurized.

NASM's Me 262, photographed following restoration in 1979.

Arado Ar 234 B2 Blitz

By 1940, Nazi Germany's aviation engineers were developing jet engines and planning a variety of aircraft in which to employ them. The Arado aircraft company was designing a high-wing reconnaissance aircraft that was to be powered by two BMW 003 jet engines. In April 1942, following engine supply problems and a series of changing orders and requirements, Arado was authorized to begin construction of six prototypes powered by Junkers Jumo 004 jet engines. The first prototype flew on July 30, 1943.

The low thrust produced by early German jet engines forced Arado engineers to design an aircraft with minimal frontal area and low fuselage and wing drag. Designed for a single crewman, the resulting Arado 234 had a slim, nearly round fuselage with a flush-fitting canopy. The wings were relatively short and had a very thin cross section. One jet engine was mounted under each wing. To minimize weight, save room for internal fuel tanks, and keep the fuselage slim, designers dispensed with conventional landing gear and designed the Ar 234 to take off from a detachable dolly. (The dolly was dropped by parachute for the next takeoff.) A skid extended along the bottom of the fuselage for landing.

Early flight tests proceeded better than expected and, recognizing the potential of a fast jet-powered bomber, the Luftwaffe issued design orders to adopt conventional landing gear and to modify the aircraft as a bomber. Arado widened the fuselage slightly to accommodate the main landing gear, added a semi-recessed bomb bay, and installed a bomb sight and an autopilot. During a normal level bombing run, the pilot turned on the autopilot,

The Museum's Ar 234, photographed at the completion of its U.S. flight evaluations.

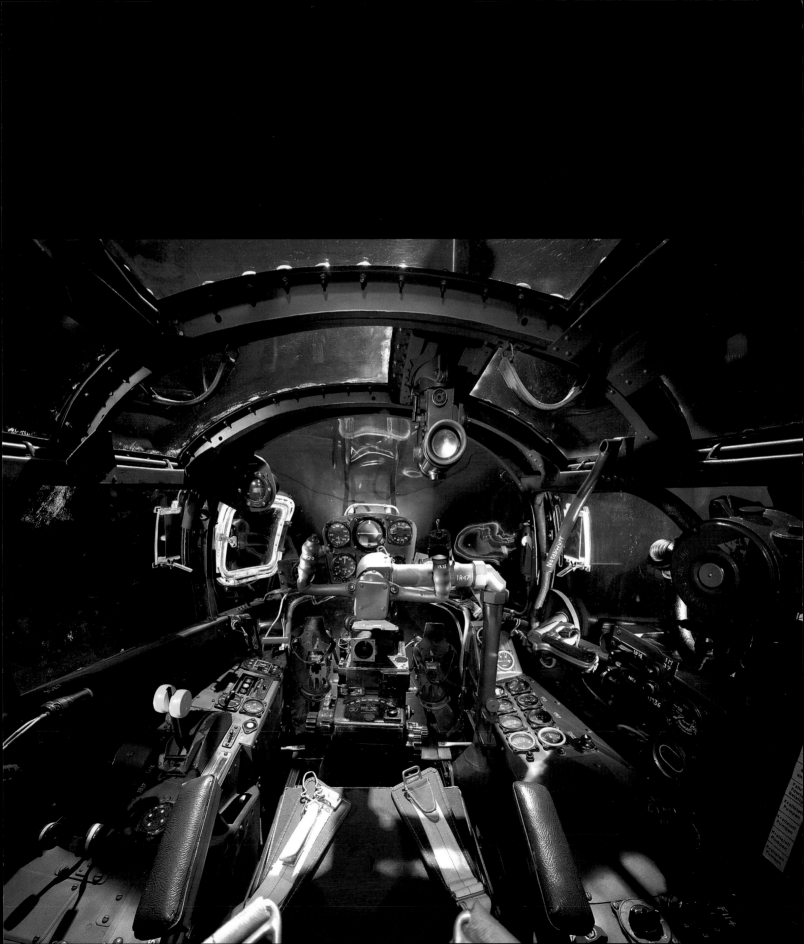

swung the control column out of the way, and leaned forward to use the sight. A periscope mounted above and slightly to the pilot's right (above) was originally provided for sighting two fixed, rear-firing cannons, but those weapons were never installed. The periscope was still of some use when checking to the rear or, when switched forward, as a bomb sight for the rare glide-bombing run. A space in the aft fuselage carried two cameras for reconnaissance missions. Also added was a rocket-assisted takeoff unit that could be mounted on the underwing just outside each jet engine. Each RATO unit provided 1,100 pounds (500 kg) of thrust for thirty seconds to help the aircraft get airborne. The rockets were then jettisoned, parachuted to earth, recovered, re-serviced and used again.

The resulting aircraft was designated the Ar 234 B and became the world's first jet bomber and reconnais-sance aircraft. The Ar 234 was more successful as a reconnaissance platform than in its bomber role, mainly because it was employed so late in the War and due to its speed, over 460 mph at 20,000 feet (736 km/h at 6,000 m), and a service ceiling of 32,000 feet (9,600 m). Ar 234s continued to fly unabated over England, France, Italy, and Holland up to the closing weeks of the War. They were vulnerable only when taking off or landing, when they lacked the speed necessary for evasion.

The aircraft's extensively glazed nose provided the pilot with excellent forward and lateral visibility. As the only crew member, the pilot was responsible for navigating and flying the aircraft, looking through the periscope, sighting through the bomb sight, and manag-ing the dwindling fuel supply for his thirsty Jumo 004 engines. The two throttles are on the left with yellow handles; the blue-gray oxygen regulator is located to the right, near the pilot's right arm; and the control yoke and rudder pedals are quite prominent in the photo. The pri-mary bomb sight, located between the pilot's knees and behind the yoke, is folded down in the photo.

NASM's Arado 234 was captured by the British in Norway at the end of the War. It was turned over to the U.S. Army Air Forces, flown to France, and then shipped back to the U.S. for testing and evaluation. At the con-clusion of the testing, it was donated to the Smithsonian Institution's National Air Museum. It was kept in storage until 1984, when NASM began a forty-one-month restoration of what is the last remaining Ar 234 in the world.

Kugisho MXY7 Model 22 Ohka

In the summer of 1944, the Japanese faced overwhelming odds as Allied Forces moved toward mainland Japan. Vice-Admiral Onishi recommended that the Japanese Navy form special attack groups to launch against the large group of American warships gathering near the Philippines. Under the Bushido — the warrior code of honor and conduct — pilots would be asked to make the ultimate sacrifice to save homeland, countrymen, and the Emperor. It was hoped that the "Kamikaze" could replicate the miracle of the "Divine Wind," a typhoon that destroyed an invading Mongol fleet in 1281.

As the special attack forces began to take shape, Ensign Mitsuo Ohta conceived the idea of a small rocket-powered aircraft to be used specifically for the special attack missions. Navy officials at the First Naval Air Technical Bureau (Kugisho) were impressed, and the Ohka (Cherry Blossom) project began. The single-seat Model 11 was designed to carry a 1,200-kilogram (2,646 lb) warhead in the nose. Three small rocket engines mounted aft gave a top speed of 350 knots (403 mph or 645 km/h) at full thrust. The Ohka would be carried to within striking distance (23 miles/37 km) beneath a twin-engined Mitsubishi G4M Betty bomber. The U.S. Navy's use of radar picket ships made the Ohka's combat debut a disaster for the Japanese. On March 21, 1945, Grumman F6F Hellcats intercepted sixteen Ohka-carrying Bettys. The entire Japanese group was shot down, with most of the Ohkas falling into the sea before

The National Air and Space Museum's MXY7 Model 22 is the only surviving jet-powered Ohka.

they could be launched. The Ohka's limited range meant the Bettys could not reach the launch point before encountering U.S. Navy combat air patrols.

To solve this problem, Kugisho developed a new model and boosted its designed range to approximately 130 kilometres (80 miles). The new version, designated Ohka 22, was modified in several significant ways. The Model 22 was to be carried by the faster Navy P1Y1 Ginga bomber, but that aircraft's limited lateral clearance meant that the Ohka's wings would have to be shortened. That, in turn, forced designers to reduce the warhead by half to 600 kilograms (1,320 lbs). A new hybrid engine called the Tsu-11, a Campini-type jet engine (similar to a modern jet afterburner) with a 100-horsepower Hitachi engine as a gas generator, was installed to extend the new Ohka's range. In operation, the ground crew would start the Hitachi motor prior to takeoff, and it would idle through the cruise to the target area and separation from the mothership. At release, the Ohka pilot would apply full power to the Hitachi and ignite a fuel-air mixture. It is thought that up to fifty Ohka Model 22's were produced, and that the

only test flight was flown in July 1945. That particular test flight was unsatisfactory, and the War ended before the Ohka 22 saw combat.

A view of the Ohka 22 cockpit reveals a very rudimentary panel with extremely simple systems that could be operated by the highly motivated but relatively unskilled pilots. Note that the control stick and throttle are made of wood — metal was a scarce commodity in 1945 Japan. Prominent and foreboding is the sight gauge in front of the windscreen. When aligned with a "pipper" further out on the nose of the Ohka, the pilot could establish his aim at the target. The red fuel valve on the left side, just in front of the throttle, allowed the pilot to control fuel flow both from the mother-ship, through a quick-disconnect line, and from the Ohka's internal fuel tanks to both the Hitachi and the crude jet engine. The vertical gauge on the right side served as a dive-angle measurement, and the red handle just below was used to arm the fuse for the warhead located in the nose of the Ohka. The ignition switch for the Hitachi and jet engines is on the right, just below the compass.

Boeing B-29 Superfortress
Enola Gay

The development of the Boeing B-29 Superfortress was as unique as its technological improvements were radical. In January 1940, with war clouds gathering on both the European and Pacific horizons, and many Army Air Corps leaders believing that they needed to undertake a long-range offensive role, the War Department published a requirement for a very long-range, very heavy four-engine bomber. The requirement insisted that the bomber carry a 2,000-pound (900 kg) bomb load at least 5,333 miles (8,533 km) at a speed of 400 mph (640km/h). By December 1941 the urgency of this requirement had increased significantly. While four airplane manufacturers were asked to compete for the contract, Boeing was considered the likely choice. Their design teams were already familiar with four-engine airplanes and heavy long-range bombers and had experimented with pressurized airplanes. Because of the urgency, the contracting, procurement and production processes, and flight-test program were greatly accelerated.

Many aspects of the new bomber were radically different from previous designs. The wing was entirely new, a design that produced high lift at low speeds for takeoff and landing, while providing low drag during cruise, enhancing range and speed capabilities. The remote-controlled defensive gunnery system, also a new concept, allowed a central fire-control gunner with computerized sights to direct the fire of the four gun turrets more accurately than conventional turrets. Although England and Germany had experimented with cockpit pressurization, the B-29 was the first aircraft with such a large and sophisticated pressurization system. This system allowed the B-29 crews to fly long high-altitude missions in relative comfort and was a first step toward the comfort that passengers enjoy in today's modern airliners.

Of the 3,965 Boeing B-29s that were manufactured, one is especially significant. The Superfortress named *Enola Gay* was one of the primary arbiters of the end of World War II in the Pacific. As a part of the 509th Composite Group, and piloted by Colonel Paul W. Tibbets, *Enola Gay* became the first airplane to drop an atomic bomb.

The B-29s of the 509th Composite Group were called *Silverplate* aircraft and differed from other Superfortresses. They were to be equipped with four fully reversible Curtiss electric propellers instead of the normal Hamilton Standard props. To reduce weight, all armor plating was removed, as were all the gun turrets except the tail gun. The bomb bay doors, which operated electrically on the B-29, operated pneumatically on the 509th Group airplanes, making them open and close much faster. This allowed the *Silverplate* Superfortress to drop its bomb and quickly begin an evasive maneuver to escape the atomic blast.

From the pilot and copilot's perspective, the B-29 cockpit differed significantly from earlier U.S. bomber and transport aircraft. In earlier models, the pilot's instrument panel was located below the windshield in front of the pilot. The bombardier was not visible to the pilot but occupied a separate compartment forward. The B-29 revolutionized the concept of crew coordination and brought cockpit resource management to a new level of importance. In the bombers that preceded the B-29, the flight crew concept was important and coordination could be the key to the success of a mission. In the B-29, flight crew coordination was not only the key to success, but it was integral to the safe operation of the airplane. For example, the role of flight engineer, a part-time duty in earlier bombers, became an important full-time job on the B-29 combat team. Seated behind

A formation of 73rd Bomb Wing B-29 Superfortresses,
photographed during a 1945 combat mission over the Pacific.

the co-pilot and facing toward the rear, the flight engineer had at hand the majority of the power plant controls and most of the basic electrical and mechanical system controls. Almost all the engine performance instruments and controls (the fuel, oil, and electrical system controls) and the oxygen and pressurization controls were also located there. In one respect, this simplified the pilot's control of the airplane, but it required a much higher degree of coordination between the pilot, copilot, and the flight engineer.

In the Superfortress, the bombardier's station was visible to the pilot and copilot. Located at the bombardier's position, and visible in the photograph, was the important Norden bomb sight. This instrument enabled the bombardier to use heading, altitude, and speed inputs to calculate precise bomb-aiming and drop timing. This Norden bomb sight (page 92) was the actual instrument used by Major Thomas Ferebee during *Enola Gay's* famous mission to Hiroshima on August 6, 1945.

Pitts Special S-1C *Little Stinker*

The post-World War II peacetime economy allowed aviators to refocus on the joys of general aviation, and manufacturers and individuals to build private aircraft. Aerobatic competition was among those joys, and the revolutionary Pitts Special S-1 was one of the first postwar aerobatic designs.

Curtis Pitts built the first single-seat Special S-1 in 1945, reasoning that the proper combination of small size, light weight, and short wingspan would result in extreme agility. Although the prototype crashed, in 1946 Pitts built a second aircraft with slightly longer wings and fuselage. Designated the S-1C, it would be flown at air shows by Phil Quigley (Pitts's friend and test pilot)

until August 1948, when it was purchased by Feminine International Aerobatic Champion Betty Skelton. Having flown a 1929 Great Lakes biplane named *The Little Stinker* since 1946, Skelton initially called the new aircraft *The Little Stinker Too*.

Skelton flew her Pitts at air shows and in competition, again winning the Feminine International Aerobatic Championships again in 1949 and 1950 (by which time the aircraft was known as *The Little Stinker* or simply *Little Stinker*). In 1951, she retired from aerobatic competition and sold the Pitts. She repurchased the aircraft in 1967 and, with her husband, Don Frankman, donated it to the National Air and Space Museum in 1985.

Betty Skelton at the controls of Little Stinker, *her Pitts Special S-1C.*

The Pitts S-1C was a small aircraft with a small cockpit — a cockpit that even the diminutive Ms Skelton found cramped. She fitted it with a canopy for comfort on cross-country flights, though this was removed for aerobatic flying. Inside, the seat was plywood with white Naugahyde upholstery and a substantial military-type lap belt. She placed a sign on the right cockpit wall warning, "For maximum passenger comfort, fasten seat belt prior to entering inverted flight." The conventional control stick, with knurled metal grip, pivoted from the floor ahead of the seat. The large housing ahead of the stick ventilated the fuel system during inverted flight — with a fuel-injected engine, there was no need for a header tank. Forward of this were two heel-operated brake pedals, and just beyond were the rudder pedals. To the left side of the cockpit was a simple throttle quadrant, and beneath the throttle was the control handle for the spring-operated elevator trim.

The layout of the main instrument panel emphasized aerobatics, with a few navigational aids for daylight cross-country flying. A simple magnetic compass was centered at the top of the panel, with the airspeed indicator below. A standard ball bank inclinometer was beneath the airspeed indicator, with a second, added by Skelton for inverted flight, mounted above. Directly on the left were the altimeter and oil-pressure/temperature gauge, with the fuel-pressure gauge and tachometer beyond. To the right were the accelerometer (g meter), the magneto switch, and the stopwatch. The red "Spin/Crash/Burn" knob (above) was, fortunately, not functional; Skelton added the feature just for fun. The shutoff lever for the fuel-injection system was mounted to the right, beneath the instrument panel and sole fuel tank.

Piper PA-12 Super Cruiser
City of Washington

One of the Piper Aircraft Company's first post-war designs, the PA-12 Super Cruiser was an improved model of the pre-war Piper J-5 Cruiser. A fabric-covered, high-winged monoplane, the PA-12 was built around welded tubular steel with wooden wing spars. Test flights began in December 1945, with the first production version delivered in February 1946.

In 1947, two Air Force Reserve officers tested the design's mettle by flying two of the new Pipers around the world. Piper Aircraft loaned a pair of secondhand Super Cruisers to majors Clifford V. Evans and George Truman. The otherwise standard aircraft carried metal fixed-pitch propellers (rather than the standard wooden ones), additional instruments and radios, and extra fuel tanks. Evans, in an aircraft nicknamed the *City of Washington*, and Truman, in the *City of the Angels*, took off from Teterboro, New Jersey, on the morning of August 9, 1947. After a minor mishap, a few adventures, and 22,500 miles (36,200 km), Evans, Truman, and the two aircraft completed their journey, landing back at Teterboro on December 10, 1947. It would be the first around-the-world flight for any aircraft with less than 100 horsepower. On September 17, 1949, Piper Aircraft founder William T. Piper, Sr. presented the *City of Washington* to the National Air Museum.

The PA-12's fuel was gravity-fed from the two wing tanks to a small header tank and on to the engine. A sight glass at the root of each wing indicated the fuel

A standard-production Piper PA-12 Super Cruiser in flight.

level, and selector valves at the lower left of the cockpit opened each wing tank. Additionally, the *City of Washington's* two rear seats were replaced with two 50-gallon (227 L) fuel tanks, increasing the total fuel capacity to 138 gallons (627 L). These tanks did not feed directly into the engine. Instead, the pilot used the red-handled wobble pump at his right knee to transfer fuel to the wing tanks and the gravity system.

With its greatly increased fuel supply, the *City of Washington* ran the danger of running out of engine oil long before it ran out of fuel. To prevent this, the pilot could transfer oil to the engine from a special one-gallon (3.8 L) oil tank situated above his right ear. The yellow-banded line from this gravity tank led down the side of the cockpit beneath the instrument panel. A small red-and-white gauge on the far lower right side of the instrument panel helped keep track of the oil level in the engine sump.

The throttle was positioned on the left side of the cockpit. The carburetor heat control and key-operated magneto switch were at the left side of the instrument panel, with the mixture control, engine primer knob, and electric starter button at the right side. Flight controls were simple: a standard aluminum-handled control stick and lightweight rudder pedals (with exposed rudder cables leading down either side of the cockpit).

Bendix provided a full complement of flight-weight radio equipment that permitted Morse code and static-free long-range communication with Army and Navy installations worldwide: a standard PAT-40 transmitter floor-mounted next to the right seat; a VHF PAT-50A transmitter on the left floor; and a PAR 70A radio and a PMR-5A spot tuner on the floor between the rudder pedals. In addition to the standard Piper-installed old-style loop antenna in the aft fuselage and a hand-wound trailing antenna reel positioned at the pilot's left eye-level, a directional loop antenna, PAAN-1A, was affixed to the top of the fuselage. A generator and a battery supplied the electrical power, with the electrical circuit breaker panel located just above the wobble pump.

Most of the *City of Washington's* main panel was standard, but three special navigational instruments bear mention. Clifford Evans designed and built a drift meter that was mounted through a hole in the lower left cockpit (the sight is now missing); the lens was outside of the aircraft. At the center of the panel was the Sperry Gyrosyn Compass indicator, which gave an accurate magnetic north reading under all conditions, without lag or oscillation. And taking the place of a standard magnetic compass, a Kollsman magnetic direction indicator was installed at the top of the windscreen. Sperry also provided a Gyro Horizon for each aircraft. These new lightweight navigational instruments and the post-war system of worldwide ground-based radio stations provided a navigational edge that allowed two pilots to safely fly light planes around the world, accomplishing in four months what would have been unthinkable only ten years earlier.

Bell XS-1 (X-1)
Glamorous Glennis

On October 14, 1947, flying the first Bell XS-1 (serial number 46-062), USAF Captain Charles "Chuck" Yeager became the first pilot to fly faster than the speed of sound. Named *Glamorous Glennis* by Yeager, to honor his wife, the XS-1 (later redesignated X-1) reached Mach 1.06 (700 mph) at an altitude of 43,000 feet (1,120 km/h at 13,000 m) over the Mojave Desert near Muroc Dry Lake, California. This flight demonstrated that aircraft could be designed to fly faster than sound, and the concept of the sound barrier crumbled into myth.

The XS-1 was developed as part of a cooperative program initiated in 1944 by the National Advisory Committee for Aeronautics (NACA) and the U.S. Army Air Forces to develop special manned transonic and supersonic research aircraft. On March 16, 1945, the AAF's Air Technical Service Command awarded the Bell Aircraft Corporation of Buffalo, New York, a contract to develop three transonic and supersonic research aircraft under project designation MX-653. The Army assigned

the designation XS-1 for Experimental Supersonic-1. Bell built three rocket-powered XS-1 aircraft.

The X-1 aircraft were constructed from high-strength aluminum, with propellant tanks fabricated from stainless steel. Nitrogen gas was used to pressurize the alcohol-water fuel mixture and the liquid-oxygen oxidizer systems for the Reaction Motors, Inc. XLR11 four-chamber, 6,000-pound-thrust rocket engine. The XLR11's four rocket chambers were stacked closely together to minimize asymmetric thrust and could be fired either individually or in groups. The smooth contours of the X-1 were patterned after the shape of a 50-caliber bullet and masked an extremely crowded fuselage containing the two propellant tanks, twelve nitrogen spheres for fuel and cabin pressurization, the pressurized cockpit (which did not include an ejection seat), three pressure regulators, and more than 500 pounds (225 kg) of special flight-test instrumentation. Although initially conceived as a ground-launched aircraft, all the X-1s were normally air-launched from B-29 or B-50 motherships. On

The second X-1 (serial 46-063) on a test flight in the late 1940s.

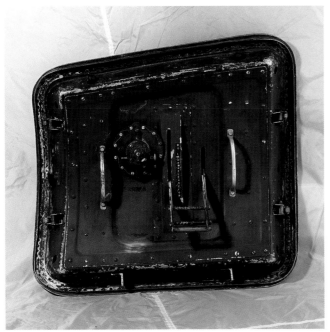

After the pilot entered the X-1 from the B-29 "mothership," crewmen lowered this hatch into position. The X-1 pilot then locked the hatch closed, and the rocket plane was ready to be released for its next mission.

The X-1's second Mach meter, calibrated for the higher speeds of the aircraft's later flights.

January 5, 1949, Chuck Yeager made the only ground-launched flight in *Glamorous Glennis*. On that flight, Yeager fired all four rocket chambers simultaneously (he had only used three on the first supersonic flight), streaked down the runway for a 1,500-foot (460 m) takeoff roll and, one minute twenty seconds later, reached 23,000 feet (2,900 m). At that point, with his fuel exhausted, he glided to a safe landing on the dry lakebed. That flight lasted two and a half minutes, and Yeager said, "There was no ride ever in the world like that one!"

The X-1 cockpit remains much the same as it was when Captain Yeager first exceeded the speed of sound: busy and cramped. The rather unique H-shaped yoke was used for both roll and pitch control, with conventional rudder pedals, barely visible at the bottom edge of the instrument panel. There was no throttle, as speed was controlled by the number of rocket chambers fired via the silver engine ignition switch at the left side of the control yoke. A conventional altimeter, airspeed indicator, and Mach indicator are also present. The Mach indicator installed on the first supersonic flight accurately measured Mach numbers to just over Mach 1. The instrument now in the cockpit measured Mach numbers up to 1.5 and was probably installed shortly after Yeager's first Mach-1 flight.

The maximum speed attained by *Glamorous Glennis* was Mach 1.45 during a flight flown by Yeager on March 26, 1948. On August 8, 1949, U.S. Air Force Major Frank Everest, Jr., flew the small rocket plane to its highest altitude: 71,902 feet (21,921 m). The Bell X-1 Number 1 continued flight-test operations until May 12, 1950, with Yeager flying the last flight. During its illustrious career, it flew seventy-eight test flights (nineteen contractor demonstration flights and fifty-nine USAF test flights) of which Yeager flew thirty-three. On August 26, 1950, the X-1 was presented to the Smithsonian Institution after a last cross-country flight a under a B-29, accompanied by Chuck Yeager.

North American F-86A Sabre

The North American F-86 Sabre was one of the world's great fighter aircraft. The first American jet fighter to have a swept wing and a moveable horizontal tail (for better control near the speed of sound), the F-86 had excellent handling characteristics and was universally liked by its pilots. First flown in October 1947, it set a world speed record of 671 miles per hour (1,100 km/h) in level flight less than a year later and could exceed the speed of sound in a shallow dive.

With the Korean War heating up and the Soviet MiG-15 appearing in the combat arena for the first time, the U.S. hurriedly shipped the Sabres to Korea to engage their Soviet-made counterpart. On December 17, 1950, in the first known combat between swept-wing jet fighters, the F-86 Sabre's excellent high-speed handling qualities and more rugged structure helped it score its first victory over the lighter and more heavily armed MiG-15.

By the end of the war, the Sabre's victory ratio over the MiG-15, depending on the source, ranged from a high of 14:1 to a low of 8:1. Even if one accepts the lower 8 to 1 ratio, it is still an impressive performance.

The F-86 cockpit, while not considered roomy, was comfortable. Many pilots proclaimed a preference for the "compact" cockpit, pointing to the ease with which the various controls, instruments, and switches could be reached. The F-86 cockpit represents a natural evolution

A combat veteran F-86A of the 4th Fighter Wing, photographed early in the Korean War.

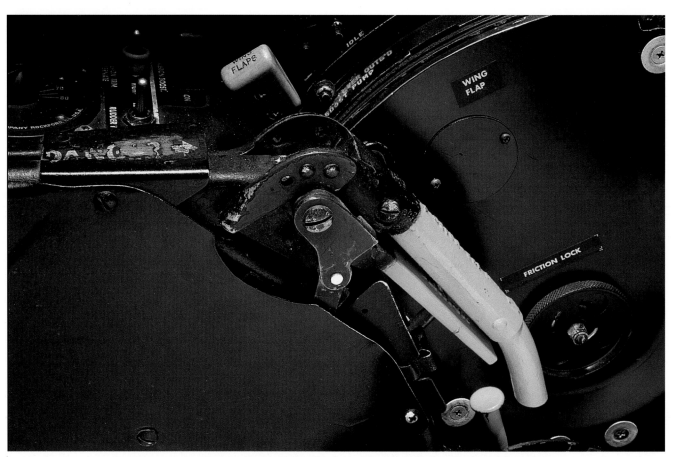

In an emergency, the F-86 pilot didn't "bail out," he "punched out" on an ejection seat.
The controls for this new advance in crew safety were mounted at the left edge of the seat.

in fighter-type aircraft, retaining many of the same basic flight-control instruments used in earlier World War II types, but with modern engine instruments, and more switches and controls for the "new" systems that were being developed. The tachometer, for instance, reads in percent instead of actual engine rpm. Instead of a manifold-pressure gauge, the exhaust-temperature gauge is prominently located above and to the right of the attitude indicator. And to the right of the tach is the cockpit-pressure altimeter, necessary with the advent of cockpit pressurization, something that few earlier fighter pilots had available. The airspeed indicator is similar to earlier models, however the higher turbojet performance is indicated by the airspeed limit needle, which is over 140 knots higher than that on the P-51 Mustang. The typical fighter control stick is still located in the center, designed to be used by the pilot's right hand, with the throttle conveniently located on the left.

There are now buttons for pitch and roll trim (the "coolie hat" on the top) and nose-wheel steering (not visible but located at the base of the stick and pointing forward) located on the stick that weren't featured on earlier aircraft. Most previous fighters had separate trim wheels and used tail wheels (instead of nose wheels) that were tied to rudder pedals when the aircraft was taxiing. Prominent atop the instrument panel is the Mark 18 lead computing gun sight, which when combined with the AN/APG radar in the upper lip of the nose intake, the six 50-caliber Browning machine guns (three on each side of the nose), and a skilled Sabre pilot, ensured the enviable victory ratio the F-86 enjoyed in Korea.

NASM's F-86A Sabre was manufactured in 1949. It entered combat in Korea with the 4th Fighter Wing, flying from Kimpo Airfield just outside Seoul. It was transferred to the Smithsonian Institution in 1962 and was restored in the markings of the 4th Fighter Wing in 1975.

Cessna 180 Skywagon
Spirit of Columbus

First produced in 1953, the Cessna Model 180 Skywagon borrowed features from Cessna's 170B and L-19 Bird Dog Army liaison aircraft. The Model 180 was a rugged four-seat aircraft with a conventional landing gear. It was powered by a 225-horsepower Continental O-470 engine and was popular as a bush-type aircraft in the U.S. and in undeveloped areas of the world. The Cessna 180 was later modified with the addition of a tricycle landing gear to become the Model 182. By 1986, Cessna had produced over 6,000 180s and over 22,000 182s.

On March 19, 1964, Geraldine "Jerrie" Mock, a Columbus, Ohio, homemaker with three children, took off in the *Spirit of Columbus* in an attempt to become the first woman to pilot an aircraft around the world. On April 17, twenty-nine days, eleven hours, and fifty-nine minutes later, she returned to Port Columbus, having set a new FAI-certified world-record speed for an aircraft weighing less than 3,858 pounds (1,736 kg) over a distance of 23,103 miles (36,964 km). On May 4, 1964, President Lyndon B. Johnson presented Mock with the Federal Aviation Administration's Gold Medal for Exceptional Service.

The Cessna 180 cockpit included many of the standard Cessna accouterments. The instrument panel included all the basic flight and engine instruments. The yoke controlled pitch and roll, and rudder pedals

Geraldine "Jerrie" Mock at the controls of her Cessna 180, the Spirit of Columbus.

controlled yaw. The pitch-trim wheel was on the floor, to the right of the rudder pedals, and the wing-flap control, a long lever with a silver button on the end, was to the right of the seat. The large white knob in the center of the lower instrument panel was the throttle. Just to the right was a mixture-control vernier knob.

The *Spirit of Columbus* was not your average Cessna 180, however, as a quick glance at the cockpit photo confirms. The right front seat was replaced with an auxiliary fuel tank, as was the entire rear bench seat. These special long-range fuel tanks added 183 gallons (695 L) to the Skywagon's normal fuel capacity. A desktop was fitted over the right auxiliary fuel tank, providing a convenient surface for charts and in-flight planning. The fuel switching and metering console, along the right edge of the cockpit outboard of the desktop, could be reached easily from the pilot's seat. The *Spirit of Columbus* was also equipped with twin Bendix ADFs

(Automatic Direction Finders, to the lower left on the instrument panel) and twin VHF Nav/Com radios (lower instrument panel, just ahead of the desktop). Atop the glare shield was the Tactair autopilot system, another special modification designed to assist the pilot during the extra-long flight legs of an around-the-world flight. Also visible, mounted on the right side of the cockpit, on the edge of the windscreen, just aft of the instrument panel, was a special mixture-control instrument that allowed the pilot to fine-tune the fuel mixture for maximum efficiency.

Jerrie Mock did not fly the *Spirit of Columbus* again after her historic flight. The Cessna Aircraft Company exchanged a later-model Cessna for the record-setting Cessna 180, which they displayed for some time at the Cessna manufacturing facility in Wichita, Kansas. Cessna donated the *Spirit of Columbus* to the National Air and Space Museum in 1975.

Douglas DC-7 *Flagship Vermont*

The final years of development of piston-powered airliners were dominated by three big American companies: Douglas, Boeing, and Lockheed. The Douglas Aircraft Company had been in business in Southern California since 1920 and had a rich history of successful products. In 1945, Douglas began marketing ex-military DC-4s, which, by the end of 1946, would equip most American airlines and several prominent foreign ones. Next came the larger, improved, and more powerful DC-6, with its pressurized cabin. The early 1950s saw further development and a breakthrough. The installation of 3,400-horsepower Wright turbo-compound R-3350 engines resulted in an airliner capable of nonstop transcontinental flights in either direction. This aircraft was the DC-7, and it entered service with American Airlines on the New York–Los Angeles route in November 1953. Later models of the DC-7 were modified with an extra 10 feet (3 m) of wing span to accommodate more fuel and make nonstop transoceanic flights a reality.

The DC-7s were the fastest piston-engine airliners of their time, with average travel times from Los Angeles to New York of under eight hours at a cruise speed of 360 miles per hour (580 km/h). Beginning in 1958, jet-powered airliners began to enter service, replacing the DC-7 and its piston-engine contemporaries. Although

A Douglas DC-7, one of fifty-eight operated by American Airlines.

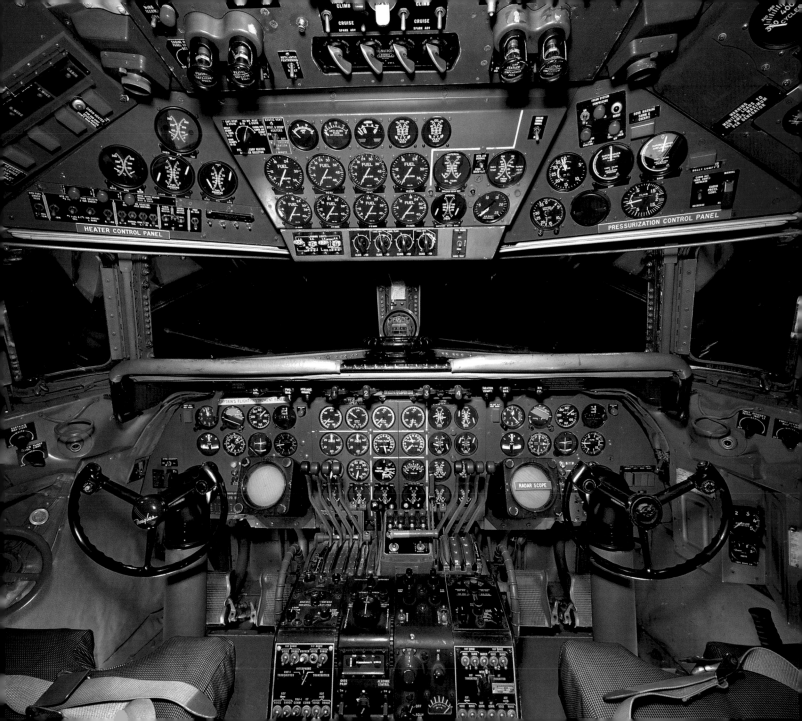

the DC-7 left major airline service by the mid-1960s, it remained in service with smaller airlines, and some were converted to freight-carrying duties.

The DC-7 flight deck accommodated a crew of three. The pilot (captain) in the left seat, co-pilot (first officer) in the right seat, and a flight engineer in a center seat between and slightly aft of the two pilots. Each pilot had identical flight instruments, a wheel yoke, and rudder pedals. The engine instruments, located in the center of the instrument panel, could be monitored easily by all three crewmembers. The wheel to the left of the pilot's seat controlled the nose-wheel steering and was only used on the ground for taxiing. The large, ridged vertical wheels on either side of the center console were the pitch-trim wheels, one for each pilot. The engine throttles and propeller controls were located on the center console between the pilots and in front of the flight engineer. The upper panels controlled various aircraft systems and were primarily operated by the flight engineer.

This particular cockpit is on display in the National Air and Space Museum's Air Transportation Gallery. The visible labels for Heater Control, Pressurization Control, Captain's Flight Instruments, and Radar Scope are for the convenience of museum visitors and were not part of the original instrument markings. For an interesting look at how airliner flight decks have evolved over the years, compare the DC-7 cockpit of the 1950s to the cockpit of the Airbus A320 of the late 1980s and early 1990s.

American Airlines presented the forward fuselage and flight deck sections of the DC-7 *Flagship Vermont* to the National Air and Space Museum. During its career, *Flagship Vermont* carried 130,000 passengers approximately 4 million miles (6.4 million km) in nearly 13,500 hours aloft.

Sikorsky UH-34D (HUS-1) Seahorse

Rotary-wing aircraft derive their lift from one or more spinning rotors. In autogyros, free-spinning rotors convert the aircraft's forward motion into lift. In helicopters, the rotors are powered, providing not only lift but also thrust to the front, rear, or either side. The development of practical helicopters advanced rapidly through the 1940s, most notably through the efforts of Russian-born American Igor Sikorsky.

In 1952, the U.S. Navy ordered an advanced anti-submarine helicopter from Sikorsky Aircraft. Sikorsky designated the new helicopter the S-58, and the Navy called it the HSS-1 Seabat, or just "Hiss." The S-58 proved capable and reliable, so the Army and Marines purchased troop-carrier versions, the Army ordering them as H-34 Choctaws in 1953, and the Marines buying HUS Seahorses in 1954. (Under a 1962 joint U.S. military designation system, all military S-58s became H-34s, though each force continued to use its own nickname.) The S-58 was also popular with foreign military forces and with civil operators. Over 2,400 were produced, including 185 built by Sud-Est in France and 395 jet-powered Wessexes built by Great Britain's Westland.

The National Air and Space Museum's H-34 entered Marine Corps service in March 1961 as an HUS-1 Seahorse; it was redesignated UH-34D in October. After 3,416 flying hours with domestic USMC squadrons, it

*A Navy HSS-1N Seabat (later redesignated SH-34J) on
a test flight over Connecticut in the late 1950s.*

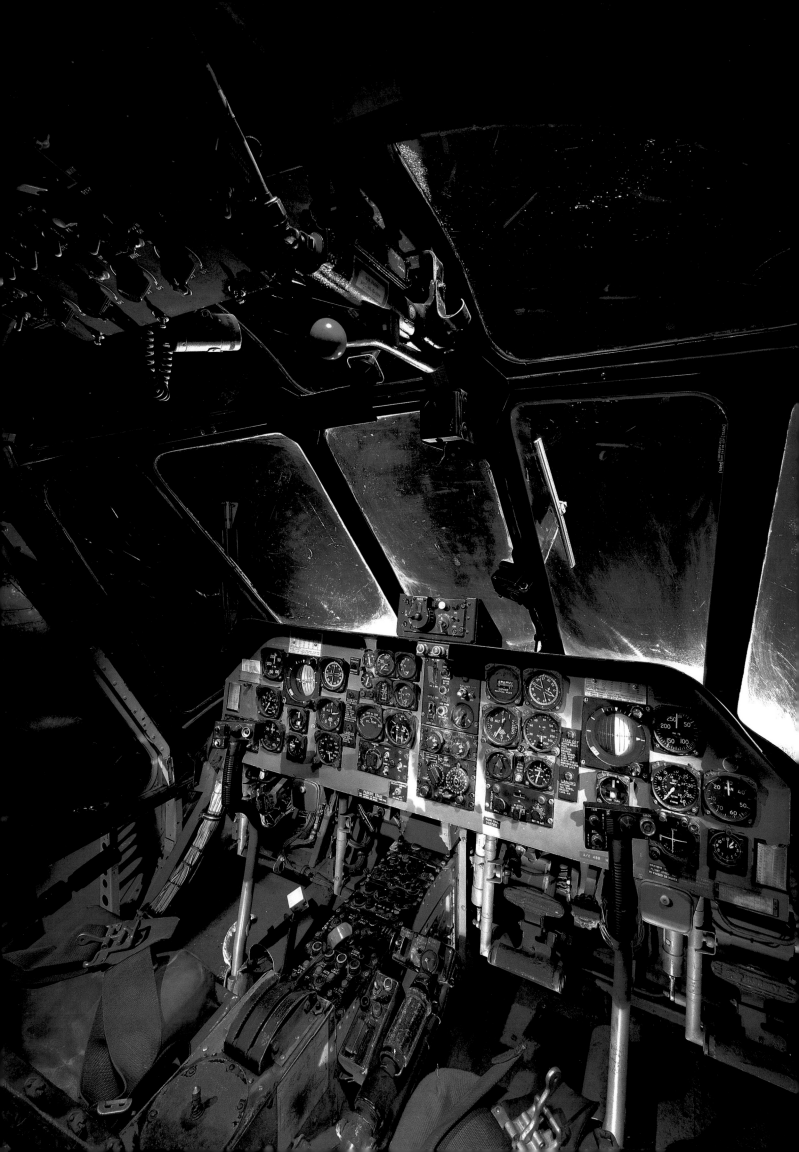

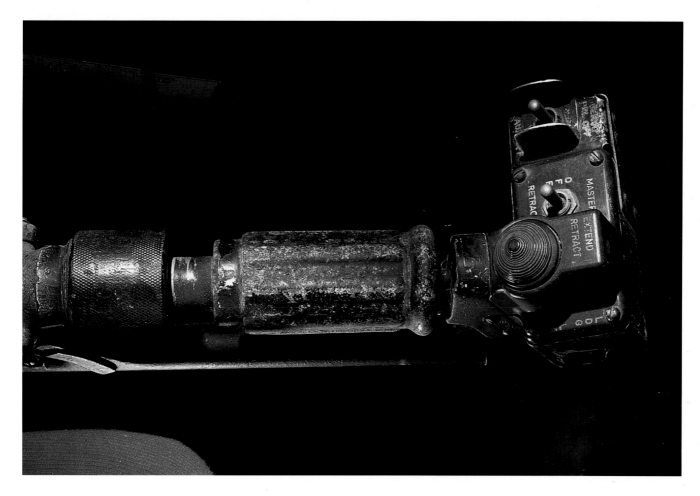

was retired in November 1970 and was transferred to NASM in 1974. It has been repainted to represent an aircraft of the highly decorated Marine Medium Helicopter Squadron 163 (HMM-163), stationed near Da Nang, Republic of Vietnam, in 1965.

The H-34's cockpit layout grew from the contemporary airplane cockpit, but with important changes. For one, helicopter pilots generally fly from the right seat, with copilots on the left; lateral seating is usually the reverse in airplanes. The helicopter pilot has three main controls and must coordinate their use. The right hand operates the cyclic pitch stick (or "cyclic"), which tilts the rotor disc. Shifting the cyclic left or right moves the helicopter to either side. Moving the stick to the front or rear tilts the nose, directing the helicopter forward or aft. The left hand holds the collective pitch lever (or "collective," see detail view). As the collective is raised, the helicopter climbs vertically; as it is lowered, the helicopter descends. A landing light and hoist control box is attached to the top of the collective, with a twist-grip throttle just below. The pilot's feet move the antitorque, or yaw, pedals, the third of the flight controls. Helicopters turn with their tail rotors and have no rudders, making the term "rudder pedal" misleading, but the antitorque pedals have the same effect: pushing either pedal turns the helicopter in that direction. The toe brakes on each pedal were for the wheeled main landing gear.

H-34 pilots and copilots sat high in their aircraft, with the diagonal driveshaft leading between them from the engine in the nose to the rotor transmission above and behind them. The seat raised for access to the main cabin below, though they generally climbed to the cockpit using external kick steps in the fuselage sides. They were provided with identical sets of flight instruments, but shared numerous engine, fuel, and electrical controls and instruments located on the center consoles and panel. Overhead, a red-knobbed lever activated a hydraulic rotor brake, which was used to release the rotor after engine warm-up or to stop the rotor in an emergency.

Bell UH-1H Iroquois, Huey

Although the U.S. Army had ordered its first UH-34 Choctaws in 1953, two years later it ordered prototypes of the jet-powered Bell Model 204 as potential replacements. Following the Army's tradition of naming its helicopters after American Indian tribes, the new helicopter was officially called the "Iroquois." The Iroquois was known briefly as the H-40, but a 1956 change in the Army's identification system led to the designation HU-1 (for Helicopter, Utility, Model 1), which the troops phonetically converted into the popular nickname "Huey." (The type became the UH-1 under a 1962 revision of all U.S. military designations, but the Huey nickname remained part of the culture.)

Over 11,200 Hueys would be built for civilian and military users, with nearly 9,500 of them delivered to the U.S. Army. The *blutta-blutta* sound of the H-1's twin-blade rotors will forever be associated with U.S. participation in the Vietnam War, where the Army used the Huey to develop its air mobility and helicopter gunship doctrines. Many early UH-1Bs and UH-1Cs were converted to gunships, or heavily armed attack helicopters, called "hogs" by the troops. The later UH-1Ds, with their enlarged cabins, were then used as "slicks," or transport and medevac helicopters. Adding a more powerful engine to the D-model led to the UH-1H, which entered production in late 1967. More H-models, including this artifact from NASM's collection, were produced than any other Huey variant.

On the ground, the Huey sat low on two parallel skids, providing crew and passengers with easy access to cockpit and cabin. The aircrew sat side by side beneath green-tinted canopy panels, with the pilot on the right and copilot on the left. Both had full controls, with lighting and engine switches atop their collectives, and microphone, trim, hoist, and armament switches on their cyclic sticks. (Few UH-1Hs carried fixed offensive armament, though many flew with defensive gunners and flexibly mounted machine guns to either side, aft of the cockpit.)

Both aircrew sat behind similar flight instruments. Each had an artificial horizon on the top row, at the center of the panel, with an airspeed indicator to the left and an altimeter to the right. (The altimeter is missing from the copilot's position in the Museum's Huey.) A radio compass sat beneath the artificial horizon, with a vertical velocity indicator to its right. The remainder of the flight instruments — including the dual tachometer, torquemeter, omni indicator, flight clock, and magnetic compass — were heavily weighted to the pilot's side of the aircraft. The fuel, oil, transmission, and electrical instruments were placed at the copilot's side of the panel, but were visible to both. The "center" console, with its radio controls, was actually mounted slightly to the left of the centerline, giving the copilot better access. The switch and blue light for the IFF (Identification, Friend or Foe) system, just to the left of the pilot's instruments on most UH-1Hs, were mounted to the right of the copilot's vertical velocity indicator on the Museum's aircraft.

A Bell UH-1H of an Army Reserve unit in Columbus, Ohio, during the late 1980s.

Dassault Fanjet Falcon 20C
Wendy

The Dassault Falcon is a French executive jet aircraft that was originally developed as the commercial version of the famous Mystere fighter aircraft. In its ten-seat executive role, the Falcon 20 shared an elite market with such aircraft as the Learjet, the Hawker-Siddeley H.S. 125, and the North American Sabreliner. The Falcon made its first flight on May 4, 1963, powered by two aft-mounted General Electric CF-700-2D turbofan engines, each with 4,250 pounds (1,915 kg) of thrust.

When Fred Smith was forming a company called Federal Express, he sought a small jet aircraft to carry small air-express packages quickly and efficiently. The Falcon was fast, with a top speed of 535 miles per hour (855 km/h), and could be easily converted for FedEx's specialized needs. Smith selected the Falcon 20, and the first two highly modified aircraft were delivered in June 1972. The modifications included the installation of a large cargo door on the left side of the forward fuselage, a strengthened cargo area floor that could accept more concentrated weight loads, increased travel of the "all-flying tail," a slightly larger nose-wheel, and higher performance brakes and batteries.

The choice proved to be a good one. FedEx was an immediate success, and within a few months, more Falcons were ordered. By the end of 1974, thirty-three of the French aircraft were flying on the spokes of the Federal Express network. One of the customs at Federal Express has been to name each aircraft after a child of a FedEx employee. This Falcon 20, the first aircraft in the FedEx fleet, is named *Wendy*, after Fred Smith's daughter.

The cockpit of the Falcon 20 was representative of the mid-1960s to mid-1970s commercial-business jet. Efficient and comfortable, it accommodated a crew of two, with the pilot in the left seat and the copilot in the right. Both pilots had a moveable yoke for roll and pitch control, rudder pedals with toe brakes, and a full

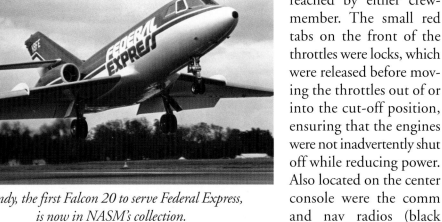

Wendy, the first Falcon 20 to serve Federal Express, is now in NASM's collection.

complement of flight-control instruments. The Falcon could be flown from either cockpit position, but because the nose-wheel steering control was on the left side of the cockpit (the gray-colored knurled wheel on the left forward side panel), ground operations were accomplished from the left seat. The throttles were located on the center console, easily reached by either crewmember. The small red tabs on the front of the throttles were locks, which were released before moving the throttles out of or into the cut-off position, ensuring that the engines were not inadvertently shut off while reducing power. Also located on the center console were the comm and nav radios (black knobs visible on the console), the air-brake lever (rear left), the wing-flap control (rear right), and the drag-chute control (the T-handle on the rear center).

The large square instrument to the right of the pilot's flight instruments was the weather radar. Just above, the vertical series of red warning lights monitored various aircraft systems, and just to the left were red fuel-shutoff handles and the fire-warning lights. The engine instruments were mounted vertically in the center of the instrument panel, with the landing-gear control handle (red wheel-shaped handle) just to the right of them. The red lever just to the right of the landing-gear control handle was the emergency landing-gear handle.

Success breeds success, and the Dassault Falcon 20 did its job so well that FedEx had to buy larger aircraft to cope with the booming demand for overnight air-express service. A fleet of Boeing 727-100s initially supplemented and finally replaced the Falcon 20s. By 1982, fewer than ten years after the Falcons entered FedEx service, the front-line package-delivery aircraft was a McDonnell Douglas DC-10, whose cargo hold could carry several Falcons. In 1983, Federal Express donated their first Dassault Falcon 20 to the National Air and Space Museum.

Mercury Capsule *Friendship 7*

On February 20, 1962, astronaut John H. Glenn, Jr., became the first American to orbit the Earth. His Mercury capsule, *Friendship 7*, weighed only about 3,000 pounds (1,360 kg), and the diameter of its heat shield base was only 73 inches (185 cm). No wonder the astronauts reportedly said, "You don't get into it, you put it on." After entry, Glenn was strapped into a fiberglass couch specially cast to fit his spacesuited shape, allowing him to more easily tolerate the high G-forces generated by launch and reentry.

The most noticeable feature of Glenn's instrument panel is the large circular periscope screen. In the original spacecraft design, there were only two small circular portholes, with the periscope providing the main view. But in an intervention made famous by Tom Wolfe's book *The Right Stuff,* the astronauts fought for and won a rectangular window in front of the astronaut's head. Glenn much preferred the view through the window to that of the periscope and found it easy to change the attitude of the spacecraft using the view of the Earth as a reference.

John Glenn "puts on" his Friendship 7 *spacecraft.*

To control the three axes — pitch (nose up or down), yaw (nose left or right) and roll (rotation left or right) — Glenn used the hand-controller in his right hand to fire hydrogen-peroxide reaction-control jets. Some of the astronauts had earlier argued for rudder pedals for controlling the yaw axis to make the spacecraft controls more aircraft-like, but lack of room, among other considerations, made that impossible. Instead the hand-controller moved in three dimensions: forward or back for pitch, side-to-side for yaw, and rotationally for roll. In the left hand of the suited mannequin in the photo is the abort handle, used to fire the escape rocket and pull the capsule away from the booster in the event of a launch emergency. In all likelihood, however, the automatic system would have reacted before Glenn would have had time to do so. The Mercury spacecraft had no rocket engines to change its orbit, so Glenn had no controls for maneuvering in space. Traveling in a fixed orbit, in a vacuum, he could have pointed the spacecraft any way he wanted without affecting his trajectory.

Three types of displays dominate the main panel. Above the periscope are a globe and clocks. The right side of the panel features gauges for the electrical system, radio, cabin pressure, oxygen supply and reaction-control system fuel. To the left and right of the panel are a number of lights; the left-hand lights were sequence lights that normally would go off in order of successful events, such as the jettisoning of the escape tower late in the launch, separation from the booster, etc. On the right are warning lights for various malfunctions.

The last rectangular light on the left, number 16 (see inset), was the subject of a famous incident during Glenn's flight. Ground telemetry indicated that the landing bag had deployed. (During landing, the Mercury heat shield dropped down on a skirt, providing a cushion when the capsule hit the ocean.) If the landing bag latches had opened, only the straps fixing the retro-rocket package to the spacecraft would have held the heat shield in place. In fact, instrumentation was at fault, but to test the landing bag, Mission Control asked Glenn to toggle the switch to the left of the light to the "auto" position and see if the light came on. It did not. Still, Mission Control was so worried that Glenn might burn up on reentry that they asked him to override the automatic retrorocket jettison by turning off the second switch on the far upper left. Glenn came through in fine shape, but the reentry was spectacular and worrying, with the retrorocket package breaking off in large flaming chunks. Glenn splashed down in the Atlantic after three orbits, a little fewer than five hours from launch.

Michael J. Neufeld • Curator, Space History Division

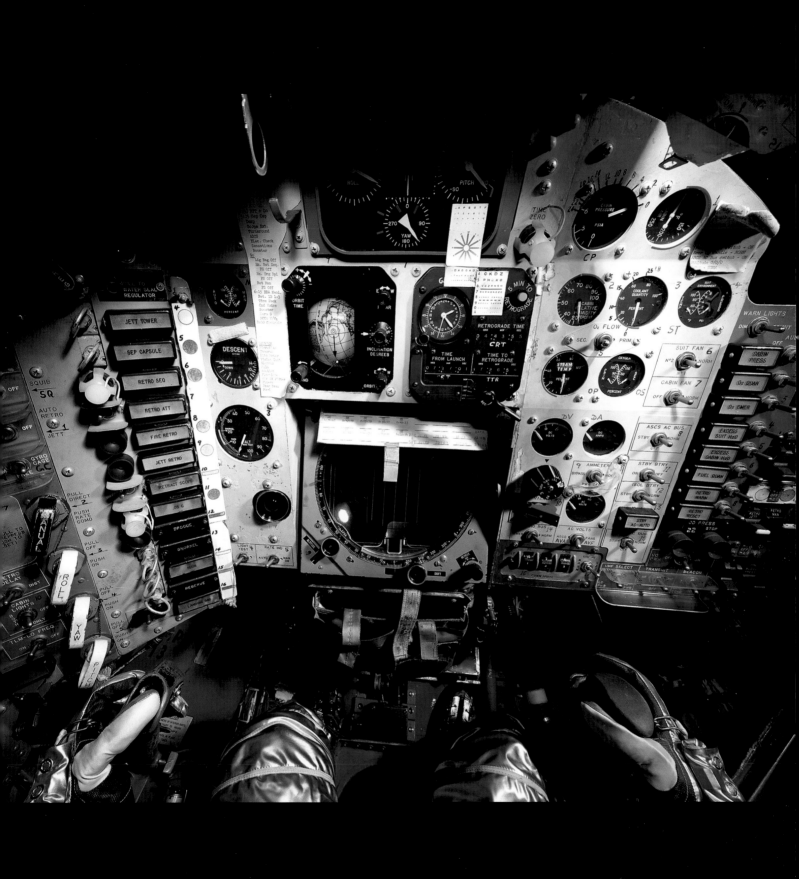

Gemini VII

Imagine spending two weeks with someone in a cockpit the size of the front half of an old Volkswagen Beetle. That was the grueling experience of Frank Borman and James Lovell, the Gemini VII astronauts. Their fourteen-day mission in December 1965 was the longest flight of the two-man Gemini program, whose objective was to demonstrate the medical feasibility of living in zero gravity for a period equaling the longest conceivable Apollo lunar landing expedition. However, because the unmanned Agena target vehicle for Gemini VI failed to reach orbit two months earlier, Gemini VII became the target for a rendezvous with Gemini VI, piloted by Walter Schirra and Thomas Stafford. Launched on December 15, eleven days after Borman and Lovell,

The Gemini VII spacecraft, photographed from Gemini VI in December 1965.

Schirra and Stafford piloted their spacecraft within a foot of Gemini VII, took spectacular pictures, and then splashed down in the ocean a day later.

Although the Gemini spacecraft began as an enlarged Mercury capsule and was built by the same contractor (McDonnell Aircraft of St. Louis, Missouri), the cockpit appears more aircraft-like. Indeed, the Gemini could maneuver in orbit to carry out a rendezvous, whereas the Mercury could change its attitude (orientation) in space but not its orbit. In addition to the attitude-control stick in the middle of the Gemini cockpit (see inset), which the astronauts used to pitch, roll, or yaw the vehicle with the reaction-control jets, there were two maneuver-controllers for firing small rocket engines to thrust forward or backward, left or right, and up or down. The commander's plunger-like maneuver-controller stick folded up under the left-hand console, and the pilot's was on the right-hand wall, but both are now missing from Gemini VII. A unique aspect of the Gemini is that the astronauts shared the single attitude-control stick in the middle. The commander and pilot had to learn to fly with opposite hands, and when some of the pilots, such as James Lovell, flew as commanders on later Gemini missions, they had to learn to switch hands.

In the center of each astronaut's main console was the "eight ball," an attitude reference device that looks like an aircraft's artificial horizon but was capable of displaying the attitude of the spacecraft in all three dimensions simultaneously. The "eight balls" were driven by a gyroscopic inertial platform that provided a continuous reference as to the direction the spacecraft was pointing and that measured any accelerations on the spacecraft from maneuvers in orbit. Under the left-hand "eight ball" is an instrument that gave the commander a readout of the spacecraft's changes in velocity in the three directions, measured in feet per second. In the right-hand seat, Gemini pilots had the first digital computer used on an American spacecraft. In the lower right corner of the panel is the ten-number keypad for the computer, and under the "eight ball" is the box for entering commands and receiving numerical data. The computer had discrete transistors, as integrated-circuit technology was still in development.

Under the pilot's main console on the right, there is a zippered storage pouch that gives an inkling of the severe stowage problem that Borman and Lovell faced. They not only had to find places to store concentrated food for two weeks, plus many other necessities, they also had to find a place to stow the garbage. Gemini had ejection seats for escape in the event of a launch emergency, unlike Mercury and Apollo, and the astronauts found that they could stuff discarded wrappers behind the seats. For the first week, they put the packaging behind Borman's seat, and for the next week behind Lovell's. By the end of the mission, to compound not having shaved or showered for two weeks, the two astronauts found themselves living inside a flying garbage can.

Michael J. Neufeld
Curator, Space History Division

Lockheed SR-71A Blackbird

Developed as a follow-up to the U-2, the SR-71 was created at the world-famous Lockheed "Skunk Works" under the guidance of aeronautical genius Kelly Johnson. The Blackbird, which first flew in December 1964, was retired by the Air Force first in 1990 and again in 1998. It remains the highest and fastest flying turbojet aircraft in history. It was designed to operate most efficiently at altitudes above 80,000 feet (24,385 m) and at speeds in excess of Mach 3, over 2,000 miles per hour (3,220 km/h). The two crewmembers, pilot in the front cockpit and reconnaissance systems officer/navigator in the rear cockpit, wear full pressure suits, sometimes appearing more like astronauts than aviators. But, in fact, this "faster than a speeding bullet" craft is all airplane, and the altitude and speed records that it holds,

85,086 feet (25,934 m) and 2,193 miles per hour (3,529 km/h), may never be challenged.

The SR-71 is actually a third-generation Blackbird. The first generation, known as the A-12, was a single-seat aircraft slightly smaller than the SR-71. The second-generation Blackbird was known as the YF-12. Designed as a supersonic interceptor with a two-person crew, it never went into production and only three service test models were built. The third generation, the SR-71, became Kelly Johnson's most famous progeny. An unarmed reconnaissance airplane, it was capable of imaging over 100,000 square miles in one hour while its electronic sensors gathered radio and radar signals, providing unequaled synoptic target coverage.

This *Star Wars* image is quickly dispelled as one views

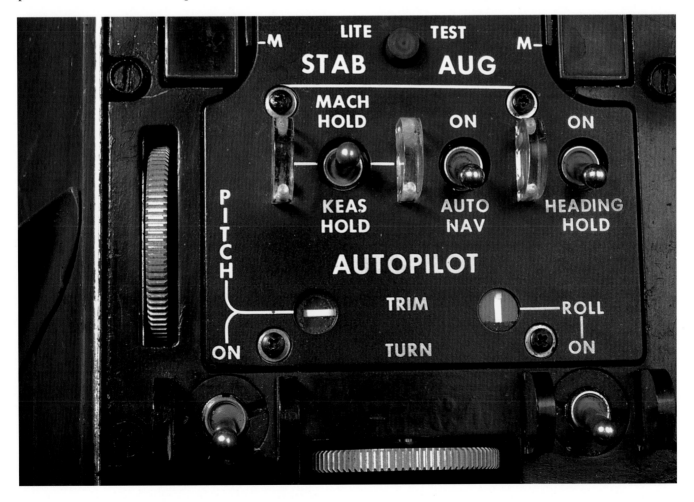

Following mid-air refueling, a Blackbird drops away from its tanker.

the Blackbird pilot's cockpit. Its early- to mid-1960s technology belies its performance capabilities. The majority of the instruments are "round gauges." Very few digital instruments are present, the main one being the triple display instrument (TDI) just to the left of the horizontal situation indicator and below the airspeed indicator. The TDI gives the pilot information from the aircraft air data computer in the form of knots equivalent airspeed (KEAS), altitude, and Mach number, all in a digital format. The pilot uses this information for very precise aircraft control.

The flight controls on the Blackbird are conventional and similar to those of the 1960s-era fighter: center control stick, rudder pedals, and two throttles on the left side panel. While the aircraft could be, and was routinely, hand-flown at maximum speed and altitude, it has an excellent autopilot. During actual reconnaissance missions, the autopilot would be the primary means of controlling the aircraft so as to provide the most stable platform possible for the imaging sensors. The autopilot controls (inset), on the right side panel, consist of two main toggle switches that engage the system in pitch and roll, two large finger-wheels that could be used to

actually control the Blackbird's pitch and roll with a single finger, and three sub-system toggle switches (Mach/KEAS hold, auto-nav, and heading hold). Normally, during supersonic cruise the pitch would be controlled using the autopilot pitch trim finger-wheel, and the roll would be controlled using auto-nav, which would receive a signal from the aircraft's astro-inertial navigation system. The pilot could precisely control Mach number to 1/100 of a Mach (i.e., 3.15), and the roll autopilot in the auto-nav mode maintained desired ground track within 1/10 of a mile during extended cruise at speeds over 2,000 miles per hour (3,220 km/h).

The Museum's SR-71, #972, flew its first flight on December 12, 1966. During its 24-year career, it flew 2,801.1 hours, many highly important reconnaissance missions, and set numerous world speed records. The Museum's Blackbird holds the flying time records from New York to London (1 hour, 54 minutes), London to Los Angeles (3 hours, 47 minutes), U.S. coast-to-coast (1 hour, 8 minutes), and Los Angeles to Washington, DC (64 minutes). The last two records were set on March 6, 1990, as the aircraft retired to NASM.

Apollo Lunar Module LM-2

Other than in airships, there are few situations in which pilots stand at the controls, but that was how the astronauts descended to and launched from the Moon in the Lunar Module (LM, pronounced "Lem"). During critical phases while in the zero gravity of lunar orbit, the astronauts wore full spacesuits and anchored themselves to the floor with cable-and-pulley restraints. The cabin of the LM was large compared to those of earlier spacecraft; the astronauts had to be able to put on and take off their spacesuits and the life-support-system backpacks they would wear on the lunar surface. In addition, without seats they could get much closer to the large triangular windows that afforded the best view of the lunar surface. The most dangerous period was the last phase of the descent, when the LM's ability to maneuver and hover greatly improved its chances of finding a safe landing spot, and its greater visibility further assured its safety.

LM-5 Eagle, the lunar module for Apollo 11's successful 1969 Moon landing.

Grumman Aircraft built LM-2, the second Lunar Module, for an unmanned test in Earth orbit, but when LM-1 worked perfectly, the LM-2 mission was cancelled. One of only two complete LMs in existence, it has been reconfigured to resemble LM-5 *Eagle*, the Apollo 11 craft that took Neil Armstrong and Buzz Aldrin to their first successful manned landing on another world. As in the Gemini, the commander (on the left) had two control sticks: a plunger-like stick that allowed his left hand to operate the small control rockets for going up or down, backward or forward, and left or right, and an attitude controller that allowed his right hand to fire the same rockets to orient the LM in pitch, roll and yaw. The lunar module pilot (on the right) had a parallel set of sticks, though the attitude controller is missing from LM-2. Each astronaut also had a black-and-white "eight ball" in the middle of the instrument panel that gave the orientation of the LM in space.

In addition to the sixteen small control jets, the LM had two large rocket engines, one each in the descent and ascent stages. The descent stage had four landing legs and served as a launch platform for the ascent stage, which held the crew cabin and took off from the moon to rendezvous in lunar orbit with the Apollo mothership, the Command and Service Modules. Primary control over the descent and ascent engines was through the main computer, the keypad of which is missing from LM-2 (note the large square hole in the lower middle of the main instrument panel).

In case of emergency, the pilot on the right had an entirely separate computer, the Abort Guidance System, the keypad of which was under the right-hand window and next to the Stop button used to shut off either engine. In an emergency scenario, the astronauts could abort the landing by pushing the Abort Stage button, the right-hand button in the center of the commander's panel surrounded by yellow-and-black hatching. That would fire the connections between the two stages and start the ascent engine to propel the crew cabin away from the descent stage and back toward orbit. One last emergency provision is shown through the Start button in the yellow-and-black hatching under the commander's left-hand window. The ascent engine could be started with this button through a direct electrical connection if a computer failure threatened to strand the astronauts on the lunar surface. Fortunately, these emergency measures were not required, as all six lunar landings were successful. (Apollo 13 never had a chance to attempt a landing.)

Over the commander's head was a third window, used for rendezvous and docking with the mothership. With this window the commander could line up the LM and dock, though in fact the command module pilot carried out the last phase of the docking himself while the LM held steady.

Michael J. Neufeld • Curator, Space History Division

Soyuz TM-10 *Vulkan*

On December 9, 1990, three men in Sokol spacesuits climbed into this Soyuz TM-10 spacecraft and prepared to undock from the Mir Space Station. The Soyuz TM-10, whose call name was *Vulkan* (Volcano), had been attached to the Mir since the previous August, when cosmonauts Gennadi Mikhailovich Manakov and Gennadi Mikhailovich Strekalov arrived at the station. Their return flight would be a much more crowded affair. Soyuz TM-11 had arrived with its scheduled replacement crew and spacecraft. Pilot Viktor Mikhailovich Afanasyev and flight engineer Musa Khiramanovich Manarov had brought Japanese journalist Tohiro Akiyama for a brief visit arranged by the Tokyo Broadcasting Company. In order to return to Earth, Manakov, Strekalov and Akiyama had to arrange themselves shoulder to shoulder in the TM-10. Three cosmonauts packed themselves into the 4 cubic meters (141 cu ft) of the Soyuz descent module. Three custom-made couch liners cradled the men for the impact when the craft touched down in central Kazakhstan.

The crowded spacecraft interior was dominated by the control panel. Instruments were arranged around the pilot, who was seated in the center couch, slightly above the other crew members. The Soyuz pilot's main assignment was to dock the spacecraft with the space station. (Though the Soyuz TM design allowed automated commands to lead it to its destination, Soviet and Russian cosmonaut pilots received bonuses for each manual rendezvous and docking.) At the center of the pilot's field of vision was the docking periscope, situated at the center bottom of the panel. It was through this periscope

Today, Soyuz TM-10 is prominently displayed in NASM's Space Hall.

that the pilot visually aligned the space station target in order to dock. To the left of the periscope, hand-controllers operated the reaction-control system, directing the small motors along the side of the craft to maneuver towards the space station. The top handle started the 9-Newton (2 lb) engines, and the lower, red handle (clearly marked "Close" in Russian) stopped them. To the left and right of the pilot were the command-signal panel and event panel, respectively. The command-signal panel offered the crew a selection of automated procedures. The event panel displayed the spacecraft systems statuses, offering warnings and cautions. At the upper left corner of the panel was the spacecraft clock with pressure and temperature indicators. At the center, above the periscope, a cathode-ray tube displayed flight information. To the right of this television display was the space navigation indicator, similar to the one that all cosmonauts, from the days of Yuri Gagarin, have used to locate their position relative to Earth.

The *Vulkan* landed on December 10, 1990. Once the crew were pulled from the craft, they each autographed the scorched ablation on the side. Although flown, Soyuz spacecraft are normally reused for training and testing. Officials in the Russian space industry offered this craft for sale at auction in 1993. The Perot Foundation bought the Soyuz TM-10 at that auction and loaned the spacecraft to the National Air and Space Museum.

Cathleen S. Lewis
Curator, Space History Division

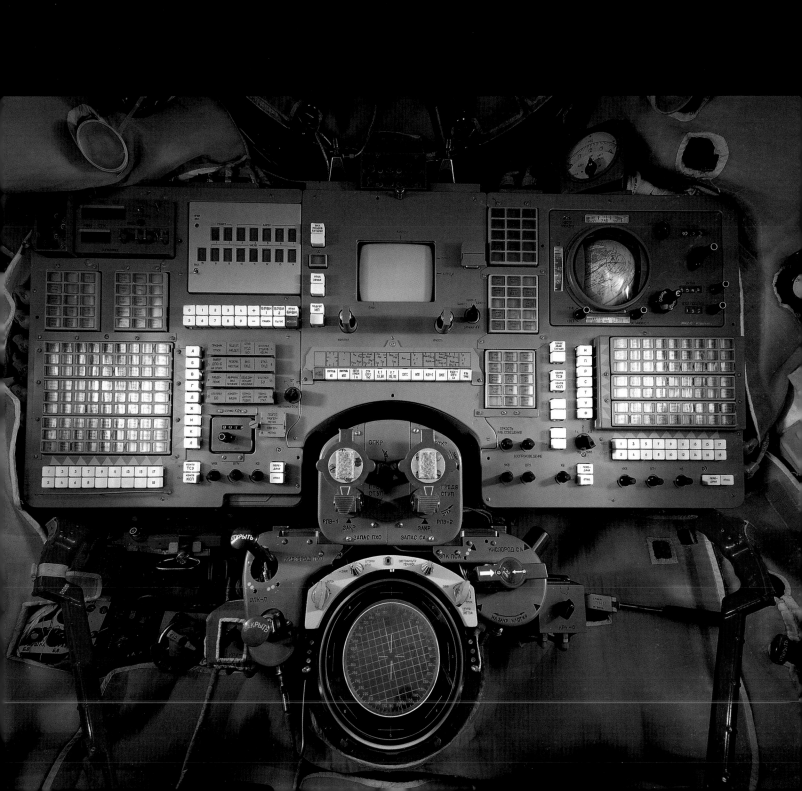

Extra 260

For over three decades, the American-built Pitts Special biplane was the world's most successful aerobatic competition aircraft, but by the early 1980s, Leo Laudenslager was challenging that dominance with his outstanding new Laser monoplane. The Laser used essentially the same four-cylinder engine as the Pitts but was capable of much higher roll rates, with much less drag. At the 1982 World Aerobatic Championships, Germany's Walter Extra, who up to that time had been flying highly modified biplanes, decided to use his engineering skills to build a monoplane that would compete with the Laser. His first effort was the very successful Extra 230, built in 1983 by his company, Extra Flugzeugbau. In 1986, Extra designed and built the Extra 260, a slightly larger aircraft that retained all of the 230's superb handling characteristics but added a more powerful six-cylinder engine. (In all, Extra Flugzeugbau would build four Extra 260s: the original with wood wings and three larger models with carbon-fiber wings.)

Walter Extra flew the original 260 until 1990, when he sold it to American Patty Wagstaff. That year, Wagstaff's performance in the Extra 260 made her the U.S. Aerobatic Team's top medal winner. In 1991 and 1992, she flew the Extra 260 to become the U.S. National Aerobatic Champion, the first woman to win this title since the men's and women's competitions were

*Patty Wagstaff's Extra 260 was photographed at Andrews Air Force Base, Maryland,
on the occasion of its donation to the National Air and Space Museum.*

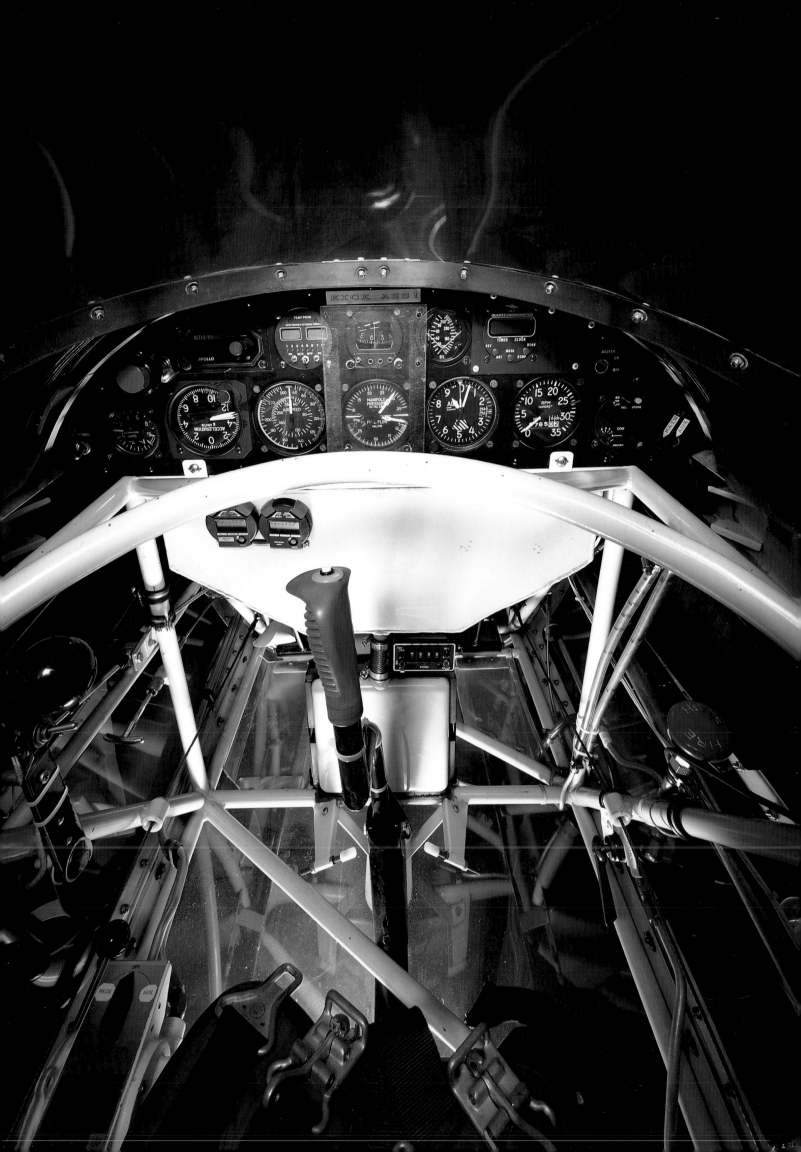

merged in 1972. In 1993, Wagstaff donated the Extra 260 to the National Air and Space Museum.

The Extra 260's compact cockpit is an excellent example of form following function. Instrument-wise, it was Spartan by general aviation standards but well equipped for world-class aerobatic maneuvering. The cockpit was dominated by a welded steel-tube fuselage frame, much like that of a race car. The pilot strapped into the seat with a five-way harness and double lap belt (the second lap belt was a precaution should the primary lap belt fail or inadvertently become unlocked during high negative-g inverted flight). A ratchet device secured the belts much tighter than normal safety belts. The control stick (with the red grip) was used for pitch and roll control, extremely sensitive and quick in the 260. Rudder pedals, just visible under the fuel tank, controlled the equally sensitive rudder.

None of the cockpit instruments — which were the bare minimum required for flight — used gyros, because gyros could not have withstood the high g-loading of aerobatic flight. The throttle and propeller pitch controls were attached to the framework on the left, with a push-pull fuel-mixture knob on the left side of the instrument panel. The fuel-tank selector valve was on the lower left of the cockpit. A 10-gallon (38 L) auxiliary tank located behind the seat could be used for either smoke oil or fuel. A red-handled valve on the lower right side allowed the pilot to switch from the smoke system to auxiliary fuel. The 10.4-gallon (39.5 L) main fuel tank was securely anchored to the aircraft frame in front of the control stick and below the instrument panel. Sight gauges for the two tanks were located at the right corner of the instrument panel and were the only "fuel gauges" in the aircraft. The large red-topped button on the right side of the cockpit activated the engine compartment's halon fire-extinguishing system.

During her short but extremely intense aerobatic program, Wagstaff kept herself oriented by using outside visual references, seen through the canopy and clear fuselage panels. The instruments she considered most important were situated across the base of the panel: two accelerometers (one flipped for inverted flight, see insert), an airspeed indicator, and an altimeter. The accelerometers still reflect the g-forces from Wagstaff's last aerobatic flight in this aircraft in June 1993. Wagstaff used a chronometer, fitted just above the tachometer, and two stopwatches, attached to the face of the fuel tank, to track the progress of her aerobatic routines. The remaining engine instruments were distributed to either side of the central instruments.

General Dynamics F-16C Fighting Falcon

Originally designed by General Dynamics to compete in a U.S. Air Force Lightweight Fighter (LWF) program, the F-16 Fighting Falcon has taken fighter performance, production efficiency, and technical innovation to a new level. The prototype YF-16 flew its first full flight on February 2, 1974, after an inadvertent first flight (getting airborne during a high-speed taxi test on January 20). After winning the LWF fly-off in January 1975, the first production F-16A was delivered in August 1978. The USAF was joined in a production consortium by four NATO countries in Europe — Belgium, Denmark, the Netherlands, and Norway, all of which had selected the F-16 as their fighter of the future. Over the succeeding

quarter century, fourteen more countries placed the aircraft in service.

The F-16 Fighting Falcon demonstrated outstanding performance capability and many innovative technologies right from the beginning. Capable of accelerating to 1,500 miles per hour (2,400 km/h), or Mach 2, at altitude, climbing to over 50,000 feet (13,000 m), and sustaining nine gs with a full internal fuel load, the aircraft was tougher than the average fighter pilot! To assist in coping with this new flight regime, the Fighting Falcon's ejection seat was tilted 30 degrees back; a state-of-the-art, fly-by-wire flight control system was introduced; and a side-stick controller was mounted,

An F-16C of the USAF's 55th Fighter Squadron, 20th Fighter Wing,
at Shaw Air Force Base, South Carolina, in 2001.

replacing the normal center control stick (above). The tilted seat greatly increases the pilot's g tolerance — a significant advantage in a combat situation. The fly-by-wire flight-control system significantly reduces weight, responding more rapidly than earlier mechanical systems. Fixed in position, the side-stick controller reacts to the pilot's hand pressure (rather than moving, as did earlier control sticks) to send electrical signals to the flight controls.

By 1988, internal and external improvements resulted in the new designation F-16C (with the similar two-seat variant designated F-16D). Among the changes was a common engine bay that would accept either the General Electric F110 engine or the original Pratt & Whitney F100. Both engines are rated at 29,000 pounds of thrust (129 kN). Upgraded avionics and fire-control systems, as well a wide variety of weapons, allow it to perform its multi-role fighter missions, including air-to-air and air-to-surface, as well as a significant standoff anti-shipping capability.

When viewing the cockpit of this "fighter pilot's fighter," or "the electric jet," as the F-16 is known, several things are immediately obvious. The aft tilt of the seat

gives the impression of reclining in the cockpit. The side stick controller is on the right of the seat, with the throttle on the left. The buttons and switches on the controller and throttle allow the pilot to activate many aircraft and fire-control systems without removing his hand.

Also noteworthy is the Head Up Display, or HUD. Without lowering his eyes, the pilot can view performance parameters and weapons display information. The pilot can read his aircraft's altitude, airspeed, and weapons conditions while simultaneously watching a maneuvering target. In addition, standard aircraft instruments can be seen in the center console between the pilot's legs. A conventional airspeed indicator appears on the left, with the altimeter to the right beside it. Below is an Attitude Director Indicator, with a Horizontal Situation Indicator below the ADI. All of these, combined with a state-of-the-art Ring Laser Gyro Inertial Navigation System and a GPS receiver, give the F-16C a superb all-weather capability, allowing it to deliver ordnance day or night under non-visual bombing conditions. Numerous individual cockpit lights — all lit for a systems test in our photo — give the pilot immediate warning of internal and external problems.

Airbus A320

In the late-1960s, world airliner production was dominated by the United States and the Soviet Union. To gain a share of this market, several European companies started a consortium named Airbus. The organization's founders believed the Americans and the Soviets had missed a vital portion of the market, and they thought they could fill that niche with a short-to-medium-range aircraft with twin-engine economy and the space and passenger comfort of a wide-body. In 1972, they built the first A300 to aggressively pursue that market. European operators at first ordered the new aircraft cautiously. Then, in 1976, U.S. carrier Eastern Airlines decided to lease four A300s, and things began to accelerate for the company. Today, the Airbus consortium produces a complete family of airliners, with over 2,500 aircraft in service, and a major share of the world's airliner market.

In 1988, Airbus introduced a new design, the revolutionary A320, a 130-to-170-seat, single-aisle aircraft incorporating the latest technology. It was powered by two engines (either CFM56-5s or IAE V2500s) and cruised at Mach .82 with a range of 2,700 to 3,000 nautical miles (5,000 to 5,600 km). The A320 is perhaps best known as the airliner that introduced the fly-by-wire flight-control system, with the pilot's control inputs transmitted to the control surfaces by electronic signals rather than mechanical means. The fly-by-wire system couples a small weight savings with a major safety feature: computerized controls make it virtually impossible to exceed safe flight parameters by exceeding g limits, maximum operating speed, or angle-of-attack limits. The

aircraft's computers refuse to accept any command that endangers the aircraft, crew, and passengers.

The A320 instrument panel is uncluttered but complete. Compare the cockpit of the Douglas DC-7 (see page 111) to the A320's advanced electronic flight deck. The A320 replaces rows of individual instruments with six fully integrated Electronic Flight Information System (EFIS) color displays. The remaining mechanical airspeed indicator, altimeter, artificial horizon, and gyro compass are included as back-ups in the event of computer malfunction. There are two EFIS displays in front of each pilot; one display monitors aircraft attitude and performance, while the other presents navigation and position information. The two displays in the center panel can be programmed to provide information related to all other aircraft systems, such as engines, fuel, and hydraulics. Smaller displays on either side of the forward center console can be programmed to present specialized information, such as takeoff and landing checklists, as needed.

The DC-7's standard center control yoke is replaced on the A320 by pressure-sensitive side stick controllers. Familiar engine throttles, flap and speed brake controls, and communications and navigation systems control heads are located along the center console, with electrical, pressurization, and oxygen systems, as well as lighting and back-up systems controls on the overhead panel. This simplification of systems has allowed Airbus to reduce its flight-deck crew to two. So successful is the A320 cockpit, that it has become standard for all new Airbus aircraft.

As of 2001, A320 production records showed 2,710 aircraft on order, with 1,467 delivered — one of the consortium's best selling aircraft. This example flies for United Airlines.

Space Shuttle *Columbia*

The first shuttle to fly in space, *Columbia* made its debut in 1981. The space shuttle cockpit reflects a major change in spaceflight philosophy from the pioneering days of the Mercury, Gemini, and Apollo spacecraft. Comparable in size to a Boeing 727 or DC-9 aircraft, the reusable shuttle was designed for "routine" transportation to and from Earth orbit by airline-like operations. Most significantly, the vehicle has wings and wheels, so it can glide through the atmosphere and land on a runway. Rudder pedals and other flight-control instruments that were unnecessary in prior spacecraft are noticeable features in the shuttle cockpit. Although the shuttle is equipped with a fly-by-wire flight control system and an auto-land system, its cockpit design presumes active control by a pair of astronauts.

The flight deck is the hub of activity for vehicle operations during all phases of the mission: countdown, launch, ascent, orbital flight, reentry, and landing. During launch and landing, the commander (left) and pilot (right) are seated in the forward flight deck. A mission specialist designated as flight engineer sits behind the center console, and another astronaut may be seated behind the pilot. Other members of the crew sit below in the middeck living quarters. Once the vehicle is in orbit, all seats except the commander's and pilot's are removed and stowed until reentry.

The Space Shuttle Columbia *lands at Kennedy Space Center.*

Crewmembers enter the vehicle through a round port-side hatch in the middeck and enter the cockpit through a square opening in the middeck ceiling (flight-deck floor). The shuttle's flight deck has both forward and aft display-control stations and windows. Certain orbital flight operations — rendezvous and docking maneuvers, altitude and vehicle attitude changes — can be performed from either station. Forward positions for commander and pilot include rotational hand-controllers on control sticks, speed brake/thrust controls, rudder pedals, forward and side instrument panels, a shared center console, and large banks of overhead instrument panels. (The seats and between-the-legs control sticks are not shown in this image.)

Some cockpit features are multipurpose, with different functions at different times in the mission, while others have a single unique purpose. For example, the rotational controllers can be used to gimbal the main engines during ascent, command the smaller engines and thrusters in space, and operate the elevons during atmospheric flight. Similarly, the lever used to throttle the main engines during ascent operates the speed brake on the tail at landing. The translational hand-controllers, one fore and one aft, are used only in orbit, primarily for rendezvous and docking maneuvers, to move the vehicle forward, back, up, down, left, or right.

The shuttle cockpit has evolved considerably since *Columbia*'s first flight. Addition of head-up displays for use during landing was an early modernization. Pictured here is the "glass cockpit" installed in *Columbia* in 2000.* Eleven full-color liquid-crystal flat-panel display units (nine forward, one side, and one aft) replaced three monochrome cathode-ray tube screens and thirty-two electro-mechanical gauges and displays. Supplementing the new electronic displays are more than 2,000 conventional displays, switches, pushbuttons, annunciator lights, and keypads.

The glass cockpit upgrade improves the amount and quality of information presented to the crew, resulting in a major increase in situational awareness. It is especially useful for showing time-critical data during launch and ascent, when an abort and quick return might be necessary and every millisecond counts. Information is color-coded by priority and presented in both two- and three-dimensional formats. Primary flight information and other data can be called up on any of the eleven display screens and combined to meet the crew's immediate needs. The new displays weigh less and use less power than the original instruments, and they make the shuttle safer, more capable, and less expensive to operate.

The shuttle's glass cockpit is similar to the systems in advanced commercial and military aircraft. Typical graphic displays include attitude director indicator, horizontal situation indicator, altitude, vertical velocity, angle of attack, Mach, airspeed, and aerodynamic control surface positions. Also displayed is information about the main propulsion system, the orbital maneuvering system and reaction control system, auxiliary power units, hydraulics, and other shuttle systems. Unlike an aircraft, the shuttle cockpit includes critical trajectory displays for ascent and reentry passage through hypersonic, supersonic, and subsonic flight regimes.

Late in reentry, at about 83,000 feet (25,300 m) and Mach 2.5, the crew activates the head-up display projections of the approach trajectory. During approach, the shuttle is a glider; the pilots have only one chance to make a deadstick landing. In concert with the automated systems, the commander flies the final approach along a 20-degree glide slope, seven times steeper than a typical passenger jet's, and then levels off to 1.5 degrees at 1,500 feet (460 m) before executing a nose-high flare maneuver for landing. The pilot lowers the landing gear and, upon touchdown at about 200 knots (230 mph or 320 km/h), deploys the drag chute to help slow the vehicle to a stop. The rudder pedals are used for nose-wheel steering and main-wheel braking. Because only five minutes pass between an altitude of ten miles and touchdown, astronauts have remarked that the shuttle descends for landing "like a ton of bricks."

* Columbia *was lost returning from space in 2003. Remaining operational shuttles are* Discovery, Atlantis, *and* Endeavour. Enterprise *served as a test vehicle and never flew in space.* Challenger *was destroyed during launch in 1986.* Atlantis *was the first shuttle to receive the glass cockpit.*

Valerie Neal
Curator, Space History Division

Photo Credits

National Air and Space Museum, Smithsonian Institution

Front cover, neg. no. 2001-984
Space Shuttle *Columbia*

Dust jacket, neg. no. 2001-2948

p. 10, neg. no. 2001-1639/26
photographers at work: SI

p. 11, neg. no. 2001-2663
the camera

p. 18, neg. no. A-26767-B-2
Wright Brothers 1903 Flyer

p. 19, neg. no. 2001-116
Wright Brothers 1903 Flyer

p. 20 (top), neg. no. 2001-1126
Wright Brothers 1903 Flyer detail:
lever to engine side

p. 20 (bottom), neg. no. 2001-1127
Wright Brothers 1903 Flyer detail:
lever to center

p. 21, neg. no. 2001-1128
Wright Brothers 1903 Flyer detail:
lever to pilot side

p. 22, neg. no. 79-4639 CT
Blériot Type XI

p. 23, neg. no. 99-40420
Blériot Type XI

p. 25, neg. no. 99-40421
SPAD XIII *Smith IV*

p. 26, neg. no. 2001-1824
SPAD XIII *Smith IV* detail:
machine gun triggers

p. 28, neg. no. 98-15200
Fokker D.VII

p. 29, neg. no. 2001-1825
Fokker D.VII detail:
airspeed meter

p. 30, neg. no. 80-12885 CT
Bellanca C.F.

p. 31, neg. no. 2001-753
Bellanca C.F.

p. 32, neg. no. A-5314
Douglas M-2 Mailplane

p. 33, neg. no. 99-40419
Douglas M-2 Mailplane

p. 34, neg. no. A-1598
Ryan NYP *Spirit of St. Louis*

p. 35, neg. no. 2001-136
Ryan NYP *Spirit of St. Louis*

pp. 36–37, neg. no. 2001-1352
Ryan NYP *Spirit of St. Louis* detail:
periscope

p. 38, neg. no. A-5172
Lockheed Model 8 Sirius
Tingmissartoq

p. 39, neg. no. 2001-117
Lockheed Model 8 Sirius
Tingmissartoq

p. 41, neg. no. 87-2501
Bowlus-duPont 1-S-2100 Senior
Albatross *Falcon*

pp. 42–43, neg. no. 2001-126
Bowlus-duPont 1-S-2100 Senior
Albatross *Falcon*

p. 45, neg. no. 2001-651
Boeing P-26A Peashooter

p. 47, neg. no. A-4587-A
Northrop Gamma 2B *Polar Star*

pp. 48–49, neg. no. 98-15205
Northrop Gamma 2B *Polar Star*

p. 50, Neg No. A-41270
Hughes 1B Racer

p. 51, neg. no. 98-15204
Hughes 1B Racer

p. 53, neg. no. A-43509
Grumman G-22 *Gulfhawk II*

p. 54, neg. no. 2001-124
Grumman G-22 *Gulfhawk II*

p. 57, neg. no. 2001-132
Grumman G-21 Goose

p. 58, neg. no. 83-2943 CT
Northrop N-1M Jeep

p. 59, neg. no. 2001-652
Northrop N-1M Jeep

p. 60, neg. no. A-42080-B
Kellett XO-60 Autogiro

p. 61, neg. no. 2001-653
Kellett XO-60 Autogiro

p. 63, neg. no. 98-15202
Vought OS2U-3 Kingfisher

p. 64, neg. no. A-42334-D
Grumman F4F-4 (FM-1) Wildcat

p. 65, neg. no. 98-15877
Grumman F4F-4 (FM-1) Wildcat

p. 66, neg. no. 98-15878
Grumman F4F-4 (FM-1) Wildcat
detail: map table

p. 68, neg. no. 72-6833
Supermarine Spitfire HF.Mark VII

p. 69, neg. no. 98-15197
Supermarine Spitfire HF.Mark VII

p. 70, neg. no. 2001-2192
Supermarine Spitfire HF.Mark VII
detail: gun sight

p. 71, neg. no. 83-14512
Focke-Wulf Fw 190F-8

p. 72, neg. no. 2001-130
Focke-Wulf Fw 190F-8

p. 74, neg. no. 2000-9418
Ilyushin IL-2 Shturmovik

p. 75, neg. no. 2001-133
Ilyushin IL-2 Shturmovik

p. 77, neg. no. 98-15203
North American Aviation
P-51D Mustang

p. 78, neg. no. 2001-2193
North American Aviation P-51D
Mustang detail: fuel tank switches

p. 79, neg. no. 2001-1393
Aichi M6A1 Seiran

p. 80, neg. no. 2001-127
Aichi M6A1 Seiran

p. 81, neg. no. 2001-128
Aichi M6A1 Seiran detail:
aft cockpit, looking forward

p. 82, neg. no. 2001-129
Aichi M6A1 Seiran detail:
aft cockpit, looking aft

p. 84, neg. no. 79-4621 CN
Messerschmitt Me 262-1a
Schwalbe

p. 85, neg. no. 98-15875
Messerschmitt Me 262-1a
Schwalbe

p. 86, neg. no. A-51417
Arado Ar 234B-2 Blitz

p. 87, neg. no. 2001-125
Arado Ar 234B-2 Blitz

p. 88, neg. no. 2001-2194
Arado Ar 234B-2 Blitz detail:
periscope

p. 89, neg. no. 2000-9387
Kugisho MXY7 Model 22 Ohka

p. 90, neg. no. 2001-1122
Kugisho MXY7 Model 22 Ohka

p. 92, neg. no. 98-15874
Boeing B-29 Superfortress *Enola Gay* detail: Norden bomb sight

p. 93, neg. no. 98-15873
Boeing B-29 Superfortress
Enola Gay

p. 95, neg. no. 95-8289
Pitts Special S-1 *Little Stinker*

p. 96, neg. no. 2001-118
Pitts Special S-1 *Little Stinker*

p. 97, neg. no. 2001-2195
Pitts Special S-1 *Little Stinker*
detail: panic button

p. 99, neg. no. 2001-121
Piper PA-12 Super Cruiser
City of Washington

p. 101, neg. no. 81-12615
Bell X-1 *Glamorous Glennis*

p. 102, neg. no. 2001-134
Bell X-1 *Glamorous Glennis*

p. 103 (left), neg. no. 2001-135
Bell X-1 *Glamorous Glennis* detail:
hatch

p. 103 (right), neg. no. 2001-1353
Bell X-1 *Glamorous Glennis* detail:
machmeter

p. 104, neg. no. 74-9688
North American F-86A Sabre

p. 105, neg. no. 2001-131
North American F-86A Sabre

p. 106, neg. no. 2001-2201
North American F-86A Sabre
detail: ejection seat handle

p. 107, neg. no. 75-13710
Cessna 180 Skywagon
Spirit of Columbus

p. 108, neg. no. 2001-122
Cessna 180 Skywagon
Spirit of Columbus

p. 111, neg. no. 98-15201
Douglas DC-7 *Flagship Vermont*

p. 114, neg. no. 2001-119
Sikorsky UH-34D Choctaw

p. 115, neg. no. 2001-2196
Sikorsky UH-34D Choctaw detail:
collective

p. 117, neg. no. 2001-123
Bell UH-1H Iroquois, Huey

p. 118, neg. no. 76-3151
Dassault Fanjet Falcon 20C *Wendy*

p. 119, neg. no. 2001-120
Dassault Fanjet Falcon 20C *Wendy*

p. 120 (bottom), neg. no. 2001-1850 Mercury Capsule *Friendship 7*
detail: floatation bag light

p. 121, neg. no. 2001-1831
Mercury Capsule *Friendship 7*

p. 123, neg. no. 2001-752
Gemini VII Capsule

p. 124, neg. no. 2001-2197
Gemini VII Capsule detail:
hand controller

p. 125, neg. no. 2001-2200
Lockheed SR-71A Blackbird
detail: pitch-trim wheel

p. 126, neg. no. 2001-650
Lockheed SR-71A Blackbird

p. 129, neg. no. 2001-2947
Project Apollo LM-2 Lunar
Module

p. 130, neg. no. 97-15882
Soyuz TM-10 *Vulkan*

p. 131, neg. no. 2001-1823
Soyuz TM-10 *Vulkan*

p. 132, neg. no. 93-5921 (3-4)
Extra 260

p. 133, neg. no. 98-15199
Extra 260

p. 134, neg. no. 2001-1826
Extra 260 detail: inverted
instrument

p. 135, neg. no. 2001-1830
General Dynamics F-16C
Fighting Falcon

p. 136, neg. no. 2001-1822
General Dynamics F-16C
Fighting Falcon

p. 137, neg. no. 2001-1828
General Dynamics F-16C Fighting
Falcon detail: side stick controller

p. 139, neg. no. 2001-1121
Airbus A 320

p. 141, neg. no. 2001-984
Space Shuttle *Columbia*

National Air and Space Museum

p. 56, Image No. 1B-01580
Grumman G-21 Goose

p. 62, Image No. 1B-47357
Vought OS2U-3 Kingfisher

**National Air and Space Museum
Arnold Collection**

p. 98, neg. no. C 20262
Piper PA-12 Super Cruiser
City of Washington

American Airlines
p. 110, Neg No. 28569
Douglas DC-7 *Flagship Vermont*

Dana Bell
p. 116,
Bell UH-1H Iroquois, Huey

Department of Defense
p. 127, neg. no. DF ST 85-06139
Lockheed SR-71A Blackbird

HQ National Aeronautics and Space Administration
p. 120 (top), neg no. 62-MA6-108
Mercury Capsule *Friendship 7*
p. 122, neg. no. 65-HC-1261
Gemini VII Capsule
p. 128, neg. no. 69-HC-913
Project Apollo LM-2 Lunar Module
p. 140, neg. no. 97-HC-824
Space Shuttle *Columbia*

US Air Force/National Archives
p. 24, neg. no. 10653AC
SPAD XIII *Smith I*
p. 27, neg. no. 7893AC
Fokker D.VII
p. 44, neg. no. 107AC
Boeing P-26A Peashooter
p. 76, neg. no. 31302AC
North American Aviation P-51D Mustang
p. 94, neg. no. 54987AC
Boeing B-29 Superfortress *Enola Gay*

United Airlines
p. 138, Airbus A 320

United Technologies, Sikorsky
p. 113, neg. no. S 25794-B
Sikorsky UH-34D Choctaw

Additional Reading

Coombs, L. F. E. *Fighting Cockpits:1914-2000*. Osceola, Wisconsin: MBI Publishing Co., 1999.

Dwiggins, Don. *The Complete Book of Cockpits*. Blue Ridge Summit, Pennsylvania: Tab Books Inc., 1982.

Fay, John. *The Helicopter: History, Piloting and How It Flies*. New York: Hippocrene Books, 1987.

Merrick, Kenneth A. *German Aircraft Interiors, 1935-1945, Volume 1*. Sturbridge, Massachusetts: Monogram Aviation Publications, 1996.

Nijboer, Donald. *Cockpit: An Illustrated History of World War II Aircraft Interiors*. Erin, Ontario: The Boston Mills Press, 1998.

Robinson, Anthony. *In the Cockpit: Flying the World's Great Aircraft*. New York: Ziff-Davis Publishing Co., 1979.

Thom, Trevor. *The Pilot's Manual 3, Instrument Flying*. Renton, Washington: Aviation Supplies & Academics, Inc., 1993.